BLACKSTONE
GRIDDLE COOKBOOK

T. A. Thompson

Table of Contents

Introduction

Welcome to the ultimate guide for all grilling enthusiasts out there! Are you looking to create mouthwatering meals that will impress your family and friends? Look no further than the Blackstone Griddle Cookbook. This cookbook is a must-have for anyone who loves cooking outdoors, whether it is in his or her backyard or at a campsite. In this post, we will introduce you to some of the most delicious recipes from our Blackstone Griddle Cookbook, providing helpful tips and tricks along the way so that you can grill like a pro. So grab your apron and let us get started!

From juicy burgers to crispy grilled vegetables, the Blackstone Griddle Cookbook offers a variety of recipes that are sure to suit everyone's tastes. Whether you are a beginner or a seasoned griller, our systematic instructions will help make your next meal a success. In addition, we have included helpful tips and tricks that will make the grilling process easier and more enjoyable. So what are you waiting for? Let us get cooking!

What Is A Blackstone Griddle?

A Blackstone Griddle is a type of cooking appliance that is typically used outdoors. It consists of a flat surface with one or more burners underneath and is often powered by propane. Blackstone Griddles are popular for cooking foods such as pancakes, burgers, and grilled cheese sandwiches. They can also be used to cook multiple items at once, making them ideal for large gatherings.

Blackstone Griddles are also known for their versatility, as they can be used to bake, fry, and even slow-cook food. They are also easy to clean and maintain.

The Different Types of Blackstone Griddles

When it comes to outdoor cooking, there is no better option than a Blackstone griddle. These griddles are designed for use with propane gas and offer a large cooking surface that is perfect for feeding a crowd. There are several different types of Blackstone griddles on the market, each with its unique features and benefits. In this section, we will take a look at the different types of Blackstone griddles so that you can choose the best option for your needs.

The first type of Blackstone griddle is the classic model. This griddle offers a large cooking surface that is perfect for feeding a crowd. It also features a built-in grease management system that keeps your food from sticking and makes cleanup a breeze.

The next type of Blackstone griddle is the portable model. This griddle is ideal for those who want to take their cooking on the go. It features two burners that can be used independently or together for even cooking results. The portable model also comes with its own ying case, making it easy to transport from one location to another.

The third type of Blackstone griddle is the Tailgater model. This griddle is perfect for tailgating or camping trips. It features four burners that give you plenty of space to cook all of your favorite foods. The Tailgater model also comes with built-in shelves and prep areas, so you can easily keep everything organized while you cook.

The last type of Blackstone griddle is the Double Burner. This griddle offers two independent burners that provide even heating across the entire cooking surface. The double burner model also comes with a built-in grease management system, so you can cook without worrying about sticking to the griddle surface.

No matter which type of Blackstone griddle you choose, you can be sure that you are getting a high-quality-cooking appliance that will provide years of outdoor cooking enjoyment.

Pros and Cons of a Blackstone Griddle

A Blackstone Griddle is a flat flat-topping surface that is usually fueled by propane. They are becoming increasingly popular for home cooks who want to be able to cook large quantities of food at one time, or who want to be able to cook multiple items simultaneously. While there are many advantages to owning a Blackstone Griddle, there are also a few disadvantages that should be considered before making the purchase.

PROS:

-One of the main advantages of a Blackstone Griddle is that it can cook large quantities of food at one time. This is ideal for entertaining or for feeding a large family.

-Another advantage is that you can cook multiple items simultaneously on the griddle. This is perfect for those who like to have everything cooked and ready to eat at the same time.

-The flat top surface of the griddle heats evenly, so you do not have to worry about hot spots or uneven cooking.

-Blackstone Griddles are very easy to clean since they have a smooth surface with no nooks or crannies for food to be stuck in.

CONS:

-One potential downside of a Blackstone Griddle is that it uses a lot of propane when cooking. This can be expensive if you do a lot of grilling or if you use your griddle frequently.

-Another drawback is that the flat top surface can be difficult to keep control of when cooking smaller items like burgers

What Foods to Cook on a Blackstone Griddle?

There are a few factors to consider when choosing what foods to cook on a Blackstone griddle. The first is the size of the griddle. Blackstone makes two sizes of griddles, a 17-inch and a, 22-inch. The 117-inch griddle is ideal for cooking smaller items like burgers, quesadillas, or grilled cheese sandwiches. The 22-inch griddle can accommodate larger items like steaks, chicken breasts, or fish fillets.

The second factor to consider is the type of food you want to cook. If you are looking for quick and easy meals, then burgers, quesadillas, and grilled cheese are the perfect choices. If you were in the mood for something a little more sophisticated, then steak or chicken breast would be better options. Lastly, if you were looking for something lighter and healthier, then fish fillets would be your best bet.

The third factor to consider is how you want to cook your food. Blackstone griddles come with both a propane and natural gas option. Propane is typiCally cheaper and easier to find, but it does have its drawbacks. Propane can give food a slightly different flavor than natural gas, so if you are particular about taste then natural gas may be the better option for you. Additionally, propane can run out quickly if you are cooking for a large group of people. Natural gas is a steadier heat source, so it is less likely to cause fluctuations in temperature that could potentially ruin your food.

Regardless of the size, type of food, or heat source you choose, Blackstone griddles are an excellent way to make delicious meals. With some planning and experimentation, you can create amazing dishes that impress your family and friends!

Recipes

If you are looking for some delicious recipes to make on your Blackstone Griddle, you have come to the right place! In this section, we will share some of our favorite recipes that are perfect for cooking on a griddle.

From breakfast to dinner and everything in between, we have got you covered with recipes for every meal of the day. We will even share some sweet dessert recipes that are sure to satisfy your sweet tooth. Therefore, whether you are a beginner or a seasoned pro at griddle cooking, we hope you will find something tasty to cook up on your Blackstone Griddle!

1.Blackstone Philly Cheesesteak

Prep time: 10minutes
Cooking time:
15minutes Servings: 4
Temperature: Medium

Ingredients:

- ➢ 1 1/2 pound steak thinly sliced
- ➢ 1 White Onion sliced
- ➢ 1/2 tsp garlic powder
- ➢ 1/2 tsp salt
- ➢ 1/2 tsp pepper
- ➢ 8 slices provolone cheese
- ➢ 4 Hoagie rolls
- ➢ 1 Tbsp. avocado oil
- ➢ 1Tbsp. butter
- ➢ 2 Tbsp. mayonnaise

Directions:

1. Turn on the Blackstone grill and heat it to medium-high (approximately 400 degrees F).
2. Place the butter and oil in the center of the grill. Therefore, that it felt, and spread out.
3. Fire up the grill and add the onions. Toss them in the oil and butter to coat them.
4. Position the onions in a more eye-catching area of the grill (front or a part where the burner is off or remove them from the grill and set them aside).
5. Position the meat in the grill's middle. It should be thinly layered. Add salt, pepper, and garlic powder for seasoning. Once the juices begin to flow, allow the steak to sear for 3 to 5 minutes
6. Next, divide the mixture into 4 equal heaps and place each pile on the grill with the pepper and onion combination on top. Add two pieces of cheese to each pile right away, and then wait for the cheese to melt (1-2 minutes).
7. Mayonnaise should be applied on one side of each hoagie roll.
8. Use your spatula to scoop and lift each pile and place the mixture onto one of the toasted hoagie rolls.
9. Serve immediately while warm and enjoy!

NUTRITION: Calories: 777Cal: Protein: 50g: Carbs: 36g: Fat: 48g

2. Birria Tacos

Prep time: 15 minutes
Cooking time: 3hours 30minutes
Servings: 3
Temperature: Low

Ingredients:

- 2 to 2 ½ pounds of boneless chuck roast cut into large chunks
- 1 tablespoon olive oil
- 3 dried guajillo chilies
- 2 dried ancho chilies
- 2 Roma tomatoes quartered
- 1 medium onion halved
- 3 cloves garlic
- 1 ½ inch cinnamon stick up to 2-inch
- 1 bay leaf
- 1 teaspoon dried oregano
- ½ teaspoon cumin seeds or ¼ teaspoon ground cumin
- 1 teaspoon dried thyme
- 1 teaspoon salt plus more to taste
- ½ teaspoon black peppercorns
- 1 to 2 cups beef broth
- For Tacos
- 12-15 corn tortillas
- 1 cup diced onion
- ¼ cup chopped cilantro
- ½ cup Mexican melting cheese such as Oaxaca
- 1 lime cut into wedges

Directions:

1. Turn off the heat, remove the beef from the sauce, and shred.
2. Heat a large skillet or griddle over medium heat. Using tongs, dip a tortilla into the top of the stew (where the Fat floats), then place it in the hot skillet. Top with some shredded beef, cheese, and cilantro.
3. Fold the tortilla over and fry for about one minute on each side, until crispy. Remove the taco to a plate or baking sheet and keep it warm. Repeat the above steps with the remaining tortillas.
4. Serve warm with a small bowl of the Birria stew for dipping.

NUTRITION: Calories: 626, Protein: 61g: Carbs: 31.8g: Fat: 17.4g

3.Classic Rueben Sandwich

Prep time: 10minutes
Cooking time: 10minutes
Servings: 4
Temperature: Medium

Ingredients:

Reuben

- ½ cup Thousand Island dressing
- 8 slices Swiss cheese
- 8 slices deli sliced corned beef
- 1 cup sauerkraut, drained
- 2 tablespoons butter, softened

Russian dressing

- 1/2 cup mayonnaise
- 2 Tbsp. chili sauce
- 2 tsp horseradish
- 2 tsp sweet pickle relish

Directions:

1. First, combine all of the Russian dressings in a bowl and set it aside.
2. Warm up the corned beef. Although it is optional, I prefer my meat hot because it is a Fatty cut. 45-60 seconds in the microwave should do.
3. Butter each slice of bread on the side that will be facing up.
4. Place cheese, corned beef, sauerkraut, and dressing on top of four of the slices. Put the buttered edges of the remaining slices of bread up on top.
5. Heat a skillet to a medium-high temperature. Place sandwiches in the skillet and cook for three to five minutes on each side, or until golden and crispy.
6. Remove and warmly serve!

NUTRITION: Calories: 657: Fat: 40g: Protein: 32: Carbs: 44g

4.Blackstone Teriyaki Chicken

Prep time: 15minutes
Cooking time: 10minutes
Servings: 6
Temperature: High

Ingredients:

- 4 Boneless Skinless Chicken Breasts diced into 1-inch pieces
- 2 Tablespoons Avocado Oil
- ¼ teaspoon Salt
- ½ teaspoon Pepper

For the Sauce:

- ¼ cup Brown Sugar
- ½ cup Low Sodium Soy Sauce
- ¼ cup Rice Vinegar
- ¼ cup Honey
- 2 teaspoons Minced Garlic
- ½ teaspoon Ground Ginger
- 1 Tablespoon Cornstarch

For the Topping:

- 2 Tablespoons Sesame Seeds
- 2 Stalks Green Onions of diced

Directions:

1. Turn on the Blackstone grill and heat it to medium-high (approximately 400 degrees F). Put an even layer of avocado oil on the grill by spreading it with a spatula.

2. Add the oil to the grill and then add the chicken. Add salt and pepper to taste. Cook the chicken for 3 to 4 minutes on each side, or until almost fully done.

3. Combine the ingredients for the sauce in a different bowl. On the Blackstone, pour this over the chicken. Stir the chicken with the sauce mixture to coat it. Cook the chicken for a further 2 to 3 minutes, or until it is thoroughly cooked and browned (internal temperature of 165 degrees F).

4. Take out and allow it to settle for five minutes, Serve the dish after adding sesame seeds and green onion dice. Enjoy!

NUTRITION: Calories: 243: Fat: 8g: Protein: 19g: Carbs: 24g

5.Blackstone Garlic Butter Corn

Prep time: 5minutes
Cooking time: 10minutes
Servings: 4
Temperature: Medium

Ingredients:

- ➢ 4 Tbsp. butter
- ➢ 1 Tbsp. garlic paste or minced garlic
- ➢ kosher salt, pepper
- ➢ 4 ears of corn on the cob shucked
- ➢ Optional: parsley for garnish

Directions:

1. Combine the garlic, kosher salt, and pepper with 3 tablespoons of the melted butter.
2. Turn the griddle's heat to medium. After the last tablespoon of butter melts, add it and spread it out evenly on the griddle.
3. Cook the corn on the griddle, flipping it occasionally, for 10 to 12 minutes. Put a melting dome over the corn to keep it from burning if you have one.
4. During the last few minutes, brush the corn with the garlic butter and, if preferred, top with parsley.

NUTRITION: Calories: 229: Fat: 17g: Protein: 3g: Carbs: 21g

6.Blackstone Nachos Supreme

Prep time: 5minutes
Cooking time: 5minutes
Servings: 3
Temperature: Medium

Ingredients:

> Olive Oil 1 tablespoon

> Ground Beef 1 lb.

> Taco Seasoning 2 tablespoons

> Tortilla Strips 12 ounces

> Water 2 tablespoons

> Shredded Cheese 2 cups

> Tomato, Diced 1/2 cup

> Peppers, Bell 1/4 cup

> Sour Cream 2 tablespoons

> Lettuce, Shredded 1/2 cup

Directions:

1. Brown the beef and taco seasoning in a skillet. Drain Fat off.

2. Include rice, water, and soup. Bring to a boil. Cook for five minutes, covered over low heat until finished.

3. Add lettuce, cheese, and salsa on top. Tostito chips should be provided for dipping.

NUTRITION: Calories: 589: Fat: 23g: Protein: 28g: Carbs: 67g

7.Griddle French toast with Texas Toast

Prep time: 5minutes
Cooking time: 5minutes
Servings: 3
Temperature: Medium

Ingredients:

- ➢ 8 slices Texas Toast
- ➢ 1 cup milk or milk substitute
- ➢ 2 large eggs
- ➢ 1 tablespoon cinnamon
- ➢ 1 tablespoon vanilla
- ➢ Butter

Directions:

1. Start by heating the Blackstone Griddle over medium heat.
2. In a bowl, mix the eggs, milk, vanilla, and cinnamon. Stir thoroughly.
3. Glaze the grill with butter once the griddle is heated. The French toast is then placed on the griddle after being dipped into the egg mixture. After cooking for two to three minutes, carefully lift up the breto check the color on the underside. Flip it over when it is golden brown. Sauté for a further 2 to 3 minutes or until everything is done.
4. Top with your preferred garnishes, serve, and eat!

NUTRITION: Calories: 176: Fat: 9g: Protein: 6g: Carbs: 17g

8. Crunch Wrap Supreme Recipe

Prep time: 15minutes
Cooking time: 6minutes
Servings: 6
Temperature: Medium

Ingredients:

- ➢ 1 pound lean ground beef
- ➢ 1 packet of gluten-free taco seasoning
- ➢ 15 ounces diced tomatoes with green chilies
- ➢ 6 large gluten-free tortillas
- ➢ 6 small gluten-free tortillas
- ➢ 6 tostadas
- ➢ 1 cup shredded Colby jack cheese
- ➢ 1 cup shredded lettuce
- ➢ 1/2 cup Greek Yogurt
- ➢ 1/2 cup salsa
- ➢ optional: nacho cheese sauce

Directions:

1. Get the meat mixture ready. Brown the beef in a sizable skillet over medium-high heat, then drain. Add a can of diced tomatoes and the packet of taco seasoning. Stir, then turn heat off.
2. Make a skillet hot. A clean pan or griddle should be warmed over medium heat.
3. Put the tortillas in a microwave. A large tortilla should be wrapped in wet paper towels. For 40 seconds, microwave the food to preheat. Before creating the next crunch wrap, repeat. If you are using ordinary flour tortillas, omit this step.
4. Put the crunch wrap together. Onto the large tortilla, spread about a third cup of the meat mixture. The meat should be covered with a tostada.
5. Wrap the Crunch. Top with the smaller tortilla then bend the corners of the large tortilla around the top to seal shut.
6. Spray pan or griddle with plenty of non-stick cooking spray or brush with oil. Cook crunch wrap for 3 minutes on each side, or until browned. Serve immediately.

NUTRITION: Calories: 497: Fat: 19g: Protein: 30g: Carbs: 47g

9. Blackstone Steak

Prep time: 10minutes
Cooking time: 6minutes
Servings: 4
Temperature: High

Ingredients:

- ➤ 4 Steaks
- ➤ 2 Tbsp. Montreal Steak Seasonings
- ➤ 2 Tbsp. Oil
- ➤ 2 Tbsp. Butter

Directions:

1. Set the Blackstone griddle to high heat for preheating (approximately 450 degrees F). For the steaks to obtain a decent sear, the griddle needs to be hot.
2. Ensure that the steaks are at room temperature and are dry. Finally, add the Montreal seasonings to the steaks (about 12 Tbsp. per steak).
3. Cover the Blackstone grill with the oil.
4. As soon as the oil is ready, put the steaks on the Blackstone grill on top of the hot oil. To obtain a decent sear on the steaks, leave them alone while they cook for 2-3 minutes.
5. Next, gently raise and flip the steak using tongs.
6. Turn the steaks over onto a different part of the grill. Next, prepare the steaks for a further 2-3 minutes.
7. Next, lower the Blackstone grill's heat setting to medium. The steak should be cooked to your satisfaction. Check the temperature of the steak with an instant-read meat thermometer.
8. After that, place a small amount of butter on top of each steak and let it to melt into the meat.
9. Serve hot, then enjoy!

NUTRITION: Calories: 588: Fat: 45g: Protein: 46g: Carb: 1g

10. Hibachi Chicken & Vegetables

Prep time: 15minutes
Cooking time: 20minutes
Servings: 1
Temperature: High

Ingredients

Hibachi Chicken

- 1 lb. boneless skinless chicken, cut into cubes
- 2 tablespoons vegetable oil
- 2 teaspoons sesame oil
- 2 tablespoons minced garlic
- 1 tablespoon grated fresh ginger
- 2 tablespoons unsalted butter
- 2 tablespoons low-sodium soy sauce
- 1/4 teaspoon black pepper

Hibachi vegetables

- 1 tablespoon vegetable oil
- 1/2 teaspoon sesame oil
- 1/2 large white onion cut into strips
- 2 small zucchini cut into strips
- 1 cup mushrooms halved
- 1 cup broccoli florets
- 1/2 large bell pepper cut into strips
- 1/2 tablespoon unsalted butter
- 1 tablespoon soy sauce
- 1/4 teaspoon black pepper
- Yum Yum Sauce for serving

Directions:

Chicken:

1. Warm the sesame oil and vegetable oil, and then turn the griddle to medium-high heat. Cook the grated ginger and minced garlic until aromatic, being careful not to let the garlic burn.

2. Quickly add the chicken and fry it until it turns a light golden brown, flipping it regularly. Stir in the butter and soy sauce until thoroughly combined.
3. To taste, add salt and pepper to the dish. Until you are ready to serve, keep it warm.

Vegetables:

1. Refill the griddle with vegetable and sesame oils, and heat until heated.
2. Include the broccoli and cook for 3 to 4 minutes, or until it is crisp and tender. Next, add the onion and bell peppers and sauté for an additional three to four minutes.
3. Add the butter, soy sauce, mushrooms, and zucchini last. Add some freshly ground black pepper.
4. Boil and toss the vegetables until they are barely tender.

NUTRITION: Calories: 458: Fat: 29g: Protein: 37g: Carbs: 12g

11. Buttermilk Blackstone Pancakes

Prep time: 5minutes
Cooking time: 15minutes
Servings: 16
Temperature: Medium

Ingredients:

- ➢ 1 ½ cups of unbleached white whole-wheat flour
- ➢ ¾ cup coconut sugar 1 ¼ teaspoon baking powder
- ➢ ½ teaspoon baking soda
- ➢ ½ teaspoon salt
- ➢ 1 ½ cups of buttermilk
- ➢ 1 egg lightly beaten
- ➢ 1 egg white
- ➢ 1 tablespoon plain Greek yogurt can also use sour cream
- ➢ Enough water to make a pouring consistency, about ¼ cup.

Directions:

1. Combine the flour, coconut sugar, baking soda, salt, and baking powder in a big bowl.
2. Whisk the buttermilk, eggs, and yogurt in a separate dish: add to the flour mixture and stir just until combined. To reach the correct consistency, add water.
3. While you heat the griddle, let the batter sit for 5 to 10 minutes.
4. Preheat the skillet, Blackstone, or griddle to medium heat. If necessary, add oil.
5. Spoon 14 cups of batter into each pancake's skillet and cook for 1-2 minutes, or until the edges are cooked and the tops are covered with bubbles. Turn pancakes carefully over and cook for an additional one to two minutes, or until bottoms are lightly brown.
6. Repeat with the remaining batter, adding a little oil between each round if necessary.

NUTRITION: Calories: 82: Fat: 1g: Protein: 3g; Carbs: 16g

12.   Blackstone Griddle Pizza

Prep time: 10minutes
Cooking time:
10minutes Servings: 4
Temperature: Medium

Ingredients:

- ➤ 2 Pre-made 12" Pizza Crust
- ➤ 2/3 cup Pizza Sauce
- ➤ 8 oz. Mozzarella Cheese shredded
- ➤ 20-22 Slices Pepperoni

Directions:

1. Turn on the Blackstone grill and heat it to medium-high (approximately 350 degrees F).
2. To cook the pepperonis, sauté them for 30 seconds each side.
3. Next, put the pizzas together. Spread approximately ⅓ cup of pizza sauce on each pre-made pizza crust. Then top with the mozzarella cheese and the heated-up pepperonis. I prepared my pizzas on a cutting board so that it was easy to slide them onto the grill.
4. Then slide the prepared pizzas onto the grill. When the bottom of the crusts, are golden brown and the cheese on top has melted, cook covered for 6-12 minutes.
5. Gently take the pizzas off the grill and set them aside to cool. They are then prepared for slicing, serving, and enjoying!

NUTRITION: Calories: 770; Fat: 26g; Protein: 33g; Carbs: 100g

13.   Griddle Patty Melt

Prep time: 5minutes
Cooking time: 15minutes
Servings: 3
Temperature: Medium

Ingredients:

> 2 pounds ground beef (85/15 is ideal)
> salt and pepper
> 1 large onion, sliced
> 2 tablespoons oil
> 4 slices Swiss cheese
> 8 slices bread (rye or sourdough is ideal)

Directions:

1. Heat a cast-iron skillet or gas griddle over medium-high heat.
2. Cut up the onion and keep it aside. Heat up the oil by adding it to the griddle. Throw the onions in and sauté them until they are cooked, browned, and tender, tossing them periodiCally. Scrape the griddle clean, then set aside.
3. Portion the ground beef into four elongated patties. You will be smashing them down when they get on the griddle for that perfect diner-style crust. You want them in the shape of a Fat hot dog, essentially.
4. Season the patties with salt, pepper, and garlic powder.
5. Cook for 2-3 minutes on one side, or until there is a dark brown crust.
6. After one flip, sprinkle cheese on top. Let the cheese melt while it is covered with a melting lid (see suggested products below).
7. Place the patties on top of the lightly toasted bread. Serve warm!

NUTRITION: Calories: 968; Fat: 57g; Protein: 75g; Carbs: 34g

14. Steak Kabobs

Prep time: 15minutes
Cook time: 15minutes
Servings: 4
Temperature: Medium

Ingredients:

- about 8 metal skewers (or wooden skewers, soaked in water for 10 minutes)
- 1/3 cup soy sauce
- 2 to 3 tablespoons olive oil
- 2 tablespoons apple cider vinegar
- 1 to 2 tablespoons honey
- 1 teaspoon freshly ground black pepper
- about 1.5 pounds boneless top sirloin steak center cut, diced into bite-sized pieces
- 1 red bell pepper, diced into bite-sized pieces
- 1 yellow or orange bell pepper, diced into bite-sized pieces
- 1 red onion, diced into bite-sized pieces
- 1 large zucchini, diced into bite-sized pieces
- about 1 1/2 cups fresh pineapple, diced into bite-sized pieces
- salt and pepper, for seasoning to taste, if desired

Directions:

1. Add the steak, soy sauce, olive oil, apple cider vinegar, honey, and pepper to a large zip top bag. Seal the bag, and then mash the contents around to cover the steak thoroughly. Put the bag in the refrigerator to marinate for a minimum of 15 minutes and a maximum of 4 hours.
2. Set a gas grill outside to medium heat, or preheat an indoor grill pan.
3. Continue adding items to a wooden skewer until it is full, starting with a piece of steak and continuing with pieces of pepper, onion, zucchini, and pineapple. Continue with the remaining skewers.
4. Add the kabobs on a grill that has been lightly greased, cover it, and cook for 7 to 8 minutes for medium-rare (145°F) and 160°F doneness, respectively.
5. Add fresh herbs as a garnish and season to taste with salt and pepper. Before serving, let the kabobs a few minutes to rest. Warm and fresh kabobs are preferred.

NUTRITION: Calories: 29; Fat: 17g; Carbs: 10g; Protein: 24g

15. Blackstone Chicken Lo Mein

Prep time: 15minutes
Cooking time:
25minutes Servings: 8
Temperature: Medium

Ingredients:

- ➤ 3/4 cup soy sauce
- ➤ 1/4 cup brown sugar
- ➤ 2 Tbsp. garlic paste or minced garlic
- ➤ 2 Tbsp. ginger paste or grated ginger
- ➤ 2 Tbsp. Sirach
- ➤ 2 Tbsp. oyster sauce
- ➤ 2 Tbsp. rice vinegar
- ➤ 3 pounds boneless skinless chicken thighs
- ➤ 1 pound spaghetti
- ➤ 8 oz. mushrooms sliced
- ➤ 1 red bell pepper thinly sliced
- ➤ 1 onion thinly sliced
- ➤ 2 to 3 carrots grated or shredded
- ➤ vegetable oil (or cooking oil of choice)
- ➤ Optional: sesame seeds or green onions to garnish, extra siracha, soy sauce, and/or yum yum sauce

Directions:

1. In a bowl, add the soy sauce, brown sugar, ginger, garlic, Sirach, oyster sauce, and rice vinegar. Whisk to blend.
2. Chicken thighs should be divided into bite-sized pieces and placed in a gallon-sized plastic bag. A few spoonful of the sauce should be added to the chicken, and then the bag should be massaged to coat the chicken completely.
3. Place the sauce in the refrigerator in a closed jar. Overnight in the refrigerator, marinate the chicken.
4. When you are ready to cook, boil the spaghetti according the instructions on the package. To prevent mush, drain and rinse with cold water.
5. Go to the griddle with the huge tray containing the chicken, cooked spaghetti, previously prepared sauce, mushrooms, red pepper, onion, and carrots.
6. For a few minutes, heat the griddle to medium-high. Add the chicken and vegetables along with some frying oil. Cook for 7 to 9 minutes, using hibachi spatulas to stir and flip the food a few times.
7. Add the sauce and the cooked spaghetti. Cook for a further four to five minutes while stirring

occasionally. Using the hibachi spatulas, transfer in little batches to the same tray you used to carry everything.

8. Serve with additional Sirach, soy sauce, and/or Yum Yum sauce as preferred, along with sesame seeds and green onions as a garnish.

NUTRITION: Calories: 139g; Fat: 30g; Carbs: 48g Protein: 23g

16.　Smash Burgers on the Blackstone Griddle

Prep time:
Cooking time: 15minutes
Servings: 1
Temperature: Medium

Ingredients:

- ➤ pounds (80/20) ground beef formed into patties, or 4 premade burger patties
- ➤ 1 white onion
- ➤ 2 fresh jalapenos, sliced
- ➤ 4 thick slices Monterey jack cheese (can also use American cheese)
- ➤ 4 burger buns (we used brioche buns), slathered with butter
- ➤ Steakhouse Seasoning (see note)
- ➤ ½ stick butter, plus extra butter for buttering the hamburger buns
- ➤ 2 Tablespoons avocado oil (or other high heat oil) for greasing the griddle
- ➤ Herb Mayonnaise:
- ➤ 2 c. mayonnaise
- ➤ 2 sCallions, finely sliced
- ➤ 1 clove garlic, pressed through a garlic press
- ➤ 1 T. fresh lemon juice
- ➤ ¼ c. fresh parsley, chopped
- ➤ ¼ c. white truffle oil (optional)
- ➤ Salt and black pepper to taste

Directions:

Smash Burgers on The Blackstone: Heat your Blackstone Griddle to medium-high heat, then drizzle a little avocado oil over the flat top of the griddle and spread it around to obtain a fresh coat of oil as it cooks up. Gather all the ingredients: the herbed mayo should be made in advance and chilled in the fridge while you cook.

Herb truffle mayonnaise Prep: Chop the fresh parsley and sCallions for the herb mayonnaise, and use a garlic press to press the garlic. Include in a small bowl. Fresh herbs should be mixed with mayonnaise, lemon juice, and optional white truffle oil (fun but not required in this herb mayonnaise recipe). Put the food in the refrigerator to cool after seasoning with salt and pepper. Slice the onion: Slice it in half while balancing it on one of these flat sides. Now take each side of the onion and slice from root to tip into thin ¼-inch ribbons. Place these slices into a bowl. Melt 4 tablespoons of butter in the middle of the Blackstone Griddle and add the sliced onions onto the cooking surface. The burners should be on medium high heat. Sprinkle the onions with the steakhouse seasoning or any seasoning salt that you like. Toss well in the butter. Cook for 15 minutes, tossing every once in a while with your spatula. I move the onions to the back. Burgers should be cooked long enough to caramelize and produce complex tastes.

Jalapenos on the Blackstone: How to Grill Them:

Cut off the stem of the jalapenos before slicing them. Cut them in half in the center. Place them in a line, and then cut each one into a half-moon. You could also choose to omit the jalapenos altogether.4 tablespoons of butter should be melted on the griddle's surface. Sliced jalapenos should be added to the butter and thoroughly mixed in. Use the steakhouse seasoning or your preferred seasoned salt to season. Cook for 5 to 10 minutes while stirring occasionally over medium heat. While you sear the burgers, move to the front of the griddle or to the side.

On The Blackstone, How To Make Smash Burgers:

Use4 pre-made hamburger patties for the burgers. With hamburger meat, you can make your own burger patties by hand or with a burger press similar to this one.

NUTRITION: Calories: 1939g; Fat: 157g; Carbs: 75g; Protein: 57g

17.   Griddle Apple Fritters Donut

Prep time: 1hour
Cooking time: 15minutes
Serving: 1
Temperature: Medium

Ingredients:

- ➤ Apples 3 each
- ➤ Sugar, Granulated 1/2 cup
- ➤ Water 1/2 cup
- ➤ Flour, All Purpose 2 tablespoons
- ➤ Cinnamon, Ground 1/2 tablespoons
- ➤ Bread Dough, 18 rolls. 1 1/2 lbs. (681 g)
- ➤ Oil, For deep frying
- ➤ Glaze
- ➤ Sugar, Powdered 2 cups
- ➤ Milk 1/4 cup
- ➤ Vanilla 1/2 teaspoon

Directions:

1. Rise the dough for frozen dinner rolls or bread loaves in accordance with the instructions on the package. Slice the apples finely and combine with the cinnamon, sugar, flour, and water in a pan.
2. Griddle the apples until they are tender. Get rid of the heat. Instead of boiling your apples down, you can use an apple pie filling from a can.
3. After the dough has finished rising, chop or break it into little pieces.
4. Add the apple filling to the dough in a Kitchen Aid mixer. To mingle, blend. Avoid over mixing.
5. On the Blackstone Griddle, heat a pan of oil to 375 degrees Fahrenheit.
6. Drop the apple fritter dough into the hot oil when it is ready.
7. Fry the fritter on one side until it turns golden brown. The fritter should be fried until it is deep-fried and the center is fully cooked.
8. Remove from the oil and set on a plate covered with paper towels.
9. Combine the glaze's ingredients in a bowl. The glaze should be used to completely coat the apple fritters.
10. Dry the fritters by setting them on a wire rack.

NUTRITION: Calories: 328g;   Fat: 4g; Carbs: 71g; Protein: 4g

18. Blackstone Pork Tenderloin

Prep Time: 1 hour 30 minutes
Cook Time: 15 minutes
Servings: 6
Temperature: Medium

Ingredients:

- ➤ 2 lb. pork tenderloins 2 1lb pork

tenderloins Pork Tenderloin Dry Rub

- ➤ 1 teaspoon kosher salt
- ➤ ¼ teaspoon black pepper

Pork Tenderloin Marinade

- ➤ 1/4 cup soy sauce
- ➤ 1/4 cup avocado oil
- ➤ 2 tbsp. honey
- ➤ 1 tbsp. Dijon mustard
- ➤ 2 cloves garlic
- ➤ 1/4 tsp coarse salt
- ➤ 1/4 tsp black pepper
- ➤ Allulose honey

Directions:

1. Combine the ingredients for the pork marinade in a small bowl. Blend thoroughly by whisking.
2. Next, add the marinade to the big bag or casserole dish that contains the pork tenderloins. Pork chops should be totally covered by massage.
3. Marinate for up to 12 hours in the refrigerator.
4. Next, switch on the Blackstone and heat it at a medium-high temperature. Add the marinade and the pork tenderloins once it is hot. Cook the pork tenderloin for 3-4 minutes on each sides.
5. Slice the tenderloin of pork.
6. Present and savor with your preferred sides.

NUTRITION: Calories: 276kCal; Carbs: 7g; Protein: 33g; Fat: 12g

19. Corned Beef Reuben on Blackstone

Prep time: 2minutes
Cook time: 5minutes
Servings: 1
Temperature: Medium

Ingredients:

- Bread, Rye, Sliced 2 each
- Butter, Softened 1 tablespoon
- Cheese, Swiss, Slices 2 each
- Corned Beef, Sliced 4 ounces
- Sauerkraut, Drained 1/2 cup
- Thousand Island dressing 1 tablespoon

Directions:

1. Before you begin, gather the ingredients.
2. The Blackstone griddle should be heated. Heat the gas grill for a Blackstone griddle on medium. Pre-heat the flat top griddle at 400 degrees Fahrenheit if using an electric Blackstone.
3. Generously butter one side of each slice of rye bread while the Blackstone griddle is heating up. One side of the non-butter rye bread slice should be covered with two pieces of Swiss cheese. The buttered side of both slices of bread should be down when they are placed on the hot flat top griddle.
4. Arrange the sliced corned beef pieces on a different area of the griddle.
5. Place the rinsed and drained sauerkraut that is not dripping on the piece of rye bread without the Swiss cheese. Soggy bread is the absolute last thing you need.
6. To ensure that the sliced corned beef cooks and heats evenly, move it around on the heated griddle.
7. To assemble the Blackstone Reuben sandwich, top the sauerkraut slice of bread with the warmed slices of corned beef. Then, top the sandwich with the other half of the bread. It will take three to five minutes to fry the corned beef Rueben sandwich on the griddle. Warm Corned Beef Rueben sandwiches should be served with your favorite sides.

NUTRITION: Calories: 850kCal; Fat: 58g; Carbs: 39;: Protein: 42g

20. Grilled Fluffernutter

Prep time: 2minutes
Cooking time: 4minutes
Servings: 1
Temperature: Medium

Ingredients:

- ➢ Bread, White, Slices 2 each
- ➢ Butter, Softened 1 tablespoon
- ➢ Peanut Butter, Creamy 2 tablespoons
- ➢ Marshmallow Crème 2 tablespoons

Directions:

1. Preheat. Griddle a meal on medium heat. Set the dial to 400°F if using an electric Blackstone Griddle.
2. Make the marshmallow sandwich while the griddle is heating up. Spread an even coating of softened butter on one side of each slice of bread.
3. After that, turn the bread over and spread an even coating of creamy peanut butter on each slice. Spread marshmallow creme evenly on the other slice of bread.
4. Spread the marshmallow fluff and peanut butter mixture over the bread, leaving the buttery edges exposed.
5. After the Blackstone Flat Top Griddle has heated up, put the buttered side of the sandwich on the surface.
6. Check the fluffernutter sandwich to see if the bread is golden brown after cooking it for about 2 minutes. Flip to the other buttered side once that side is finished. Grill until the filling is warmed and flowing out of the middle and the second side is golden.
7. Take the hot food off the flat top griddle.

NUTRITION: Calories: 49; Fat: 30g; Protein: 13g; Carbs: 48g

21.   Blackstone Griddle Glazed Carrots

Prep time: 5minutes
Cook time: 10minutes
Servings: 2
Temperature: Low

Ingredients:

- ➢ Carrots, Large, Whole 2 each
- ➢ Butter 2 Tablespoons
- ➢ Brown Sugar 2 Tablespoons

Directions:

1. Start by heating up your Blackstone Griddle.
2. Carrots should have their ends peeled and cut.
3. Carrots should be cut into desired shapes. I enjoy playing mandolins with angled throats.
4. Compile all the ingredients for the recipe for glazed carrots.
5. Put the heated griddle over your vegetables.
6. Add a few tablespoons of water to the griddle and carrots. To contain the steam, cover everything with a dome lid.
7. Prepare for roughly 2 minutes. With a spatula, turn the vegetables.
8. Keep cooking the carrots until they are barely soft.
9. Sprinkle the brown sugar and butter on top of the cooked carrots.
10. After another two minutes, flip the food to mix.
11. Take out and put the Blackstone Griddle Glazed Carrots in a serving bowl after they are finished cooking. Serve immediately.

NUTRITION: Calories: 160; Fat: 12g; Protein: 0g; Carbs: 15g

22. Recipe for Chicken Tempura

Prep time: 5minutes
Cook time: 20minutes
Servings: 1
Temperature: High

Ingredients:

- Chicken Breast. 1 Pound
- Drake's Mix 1 cup
- Water, Cold 3/4 cup
- Oil for Frying

Directions:

1. To make the chicken tempura batter, add Drake's mix and cold water to a medium bowl and whisk to smooth out any lumps.

2. Using a cutting board and a sharp knife, slice each chicken breast into long strips. Frozen chicken breast should be sliced into long strips while still partially frozen.

3. Place your Blackstone Griddle over high heat while you add frying oil to a griddle-proof pan that is between one and two inches deep. Use a digital thermometer to monitor the correct temperature and keep your frying oil at a temperature of 375°F.

4. To coat each piece of chicken breast, add the chicken strips to the tempura batter in batches and stir. Lift a piece of chicken that has been battered with a fork or tongs, letting any leftover homemade tempura batter drip back into the bowl.

5. Gently add the hot oil to the chicken strips that have been coated in Drake's. Add more chicken as needed, being careful not to crowd the pan and to prevent the birds from touching. Depending on the size of the hot oil pan you are using, you will need to work in batches. The chicken will float to the surface when it is finished cooking, though cooking times will vary.

6. Once the golden-brown crust has formed on the crispy chicken tenders, remove them from the heated oil. On a platter covered with paper towels, spread them out. While the chicken strips are still hot, serve them right away.

NUTRITION: Calories: 174; Protein: 28g; Fat: 6g; Carbs: 0g

23. Onion Swiss Pretzel Bun Burger

Prep time: 5minutes
Cook time: 10minutes
Servings: 1
Temperature: Medium

Ingredients:

- ➢ Ground Beef. 1 pound
- ➢ Onion, Sweet, Sliced 8 ounces
- ➢ Swiss Cheese, Slices 8 each
- ➢ Pretzel Buns, Mini 8 each

Directions:

1. 8 (2-ounce) ground beef balls should be made. If necessary, cut onion slices.
2. Set the temperature of your Blackstone Griddle Grill to medium.
3. The Blackstone Griddle should be coated in olive oil before adding the onions. Sauté food until it turns golden and caramelizes.
4. Put the hot griddle with the mashed hamburger balls on it.
5. Flatten each burger ball into very thin patties using a piece of parchment paper and your griddle spatula or burger press. Peel the paper from each crushed patty with caution.
6. Add your preferred seasonings to each patty once it has been crushed.
7. Butter each pretzel bun before placing it on the skillet to toast.
8. Fry the burger patty for 2-3 minutes on each side, or until it is crispy brown. Swiss cheese should be added to the smashed patty just before it is finished.
9. Construct your onion Swiss pretzel bread burger by placing the cheese-covered burger patty on the bottom pretzel bun, followed by any additional toppings and any condiments, if desired. Serve them while they are still hot and add the top pretzel bun.

NUTRITION: Calories: 434; Fat: 22g; Protein: 28g; Carbs: 31g

24. Bacon Brussel Sprouts

Prep Time: 10minutes
Cook Time: 30 minutes
Servings: 6
Temperature: Medium

Ingredients:

- 3 cups Brussel sprouts trimmed, loose leaves removed, and halved
- 6 slices bacon chopped
- 2 shallots sliced, can substitute with red onion or Vidalia onion
- 1 tablespoon olive oil
- ½ teaspoon salt
- ½ teaspoon pepper
- ½ teaspoon garlic powder

Directions:

1. Boiling water should be used to blanch the prepared Brussels sprouts for 10 minutes.
2. Heat the griddle to about 300 and 325 F.
3. Add the bacon and heat it just until it begins to crisp. The shallots are then added and cooked until just softened. Take a position to the side of the griddle.
4. Fill the remaining griddle with the Brussel sprouts, salt, pepper, garlic powder, and olive oil. Coat the frying surface by tossing. Sauté the sprouts for 5 to 10 minutes, or until browned. Combine all ingredients and toss before transferring to baking sheet or bowl.
5. You can either serve it right away or keep it in an airtight jar for up to a week.

NUTRITION: Calories: 56kCal; Carbs: 6g; Protein: 2g; Fat: 3g

25.   Salmon on the Blackstone Griddle

Prep time: 5minutes
Cook time: 7minutes
Servings: 3
Temperature: Medium

Ingredients:

- ➢ 1 pound salmon
- ➢ ¼ cup paleo teriyaki sauce
- ➢ 1 tbsp. avocado oil

Directions:

1. First, make 5 to 6 ounce filets of salmon.
2. Next, look for pin bones in your salmon filets. If any, get rid of them. If they are very difficult, try using tweezers or even pliers (make sure you only use kitchen-specific pliers).
3. Next, heat your Blackstone griddle to between 375 and 400 degrees. On my sCale, this is roughly medium high.
4. After the flat top grill has heated up, add the oil.
5. After that, add the salmon filets and cook for 3 minutes with the skin side down.
6. After the second flip, cook for 2 minutes with the flesh side down.
7. Turn the salmon back so the skin is facing up and drizzle teriyaki sauce over it. Let the salmon to cook for 1-2 minutes, or until it reaches an internal temperature of 145°F and the sauce thickens.
8. Take off the griddle, then plate.

NUTRITION: Calories: 277kCal; Carbs: 4g; Protein: 31g; Fat: 14g

26. Grilled Halloumi Cheese

Prep Time: 10minutes
Cook time:
Servings: 8
Temperature: Medium

Ingredients:

- ➢ 1 (8 oz..) package halloumi cheese
- ➢ 1 tablespoon olive oil
- ➢ Optional:
- ➢ A pinch of spices (such as smoked paprika, ground cumin, and garlic powder)*

Directions:

1. Slice the halloumi block into eight (1 oz.) slices.
2. Brush the slices with olive oil on both sides.
3. Heat a nonstick grill pan over medium heat for about 5 minutes. If you do not own a grill pan, a regular nonstick pan will work, although the fried cheese will not look as pretty without the grill marks.
4. Place the cheese slices in the pan (work in two batches if necessary). Cook for 3 minutes on each side, until crisp and browned. Serve immediately.

NUTRITION: Calories: 105kCal; Carbs: 0.1g; Protein: 6g; Fat: 9g

27.   Simple Oat Wraps Using a Cast Iron Skillet

Prep time: 5minutes
Cook time: 5minutes
Servings: 4
Temperature: medium

Ingredients:

- 150g ground oats (1¼ cups approx.)
- 250ml water (1 cup)
- Big pinch of sea salt

Directions:

1. Create the oat wrap batter (scroll for the recipe below).
2. Smooth it onto your piping hot skillet.
3. Give it a minute or two to come together
4. Flip it over.
5. Pop it into a lint-free tea towel (USA: dishtowel) or kitchen towel/paper for 10 to 15 minutes.
6. Enjoy your oat wrap as is or stuff it with your favorite ingredients.

NUTRITION: Calories: 69; Fat: 0.3g; Protein: 2.4g; Carbs: 13.5g

28.   Spinach Tuna Melt

Prep time: 15minutes
Cook time: 15minutes
Servings: 4
Temperature: Medium

Ingredients:

- 15.4 oz.. can Albacore Tuna
- 4-6 slices Easy White Sandwich Bread
- 1 cup fresh baby spinach, packed and diced
- 3 tablespoons Mayonnaise
- 1 tablespoon Dijon Mustard
- 2 tablespoons sweet pickle, diced about 1 small pickle
- 2 tablespoons butter
- 8 slices very thin sharp cheddar cheese or about 1/2 - 3/4 cup shredded

Directions:

1. Combine the tuna, mayo, mustard, spinach, and pickle in a medium bowl.
2. A griddle or sizable frying pan should be heated to medium.
3. Liberally butter one of the slices of bread. Put 2 slices of bread on the griddle, butter side down, and top with 2 thin slices of cheese, or about 1/4 of the entire amount of shredded cheese. Add a good amount of the tuna mixture on top, followed by the remaining cheese. Bread should be placed on top, buttered side up. Cook one sandwich at a time in a smaller frying pan.
4. Heat for 3 to 4 minutes or until the bottom layer of cheese is melted and the buttered side of the bread is golden brown.
5. Carefully flip your sandwich over with a large spatula, being careful not to spill its contents, and cook the second side for an additional 3 to 4 minutes or until the cheese has melted and the bread is golden brown.

NUTRITION: Calories: 448Cal; Fat: 34g; Protein: 15; Carbs: 20g

29. Cream Girdle Scones

Prep time: 15minutes
Cooking time:
10minutes Servings: 4
Temperature: Medium

Ingredients:

- 8 of (1 3/4 to 2 cups) sifted, self-rising flour (or all-purpose flour with 2 tsp baking powder)
- 1 of (1/8 cup) sugar
- 1 of (1/4 stick) butter
- 4 of (1/2 cup) milk (I used buttermilk)
- 1 egg
- pinch of salt
- 2 of (1/4 cup) raisins, or currants-optional

Directions:

1. In a big bowl, combine the butter, sugar, and egg.
2. Stir in the flour and salt after adding the milk, until a dough forms. (If adding currants or raisins, do so now.)
3. Transfer to a surface dusted with flour, fold over until smooth, and divide in half. Each half is rolled out and then cut into four quarters.
4. To test, place on a hot griddle that is set to a medium-high temperature (if some flour turns light brown in a few seconds, it is ready). When the scones have risen and the bottoms are dark, turn them over.
5. Continue to cook the scone until it is fully cooked and the opposite side is likewise well colored.
6. Remove from the heat and allow cooling in a kitchen towel before serving.
7. Serve with hot tea, butter, jam, and/or cream while still warm.

NUTRITION: Calories: 369; Fat: 1g; Protein: 10; Carbs: 80g

30.   Grilled Watermelon Salad

Prep time: 15minutes
Cook: 10minutes
Servings: 8
Temperature: High

Ingredients:

- ➤ 1 small watermelon seedless variety, if possible
- ➤ 2 ½ tablespoons olive oil divided
- ➤ 7 ounces (200g) feta cheese crumbled
- ➤ 2 cups (380g) blueberries
- ➤ 2 tablespoons orange juice
- ➤ juice from one lime
- ➤ mint leaves for garnish

Directions:

1. Preheat a griddle pan on the stovetop or an outdoor grill to high heat.
2. Remove the rind from the watermelon, cut it into wedges that are half an inch thick, and brush both sides of the wedges with 1 tablespoon of olive oil.
3. Grill the watermelon for 2-3 minutes on each side or until grill marks appear.
4. Place the blueberries and feta on top of the grilled watermelon and arrange it on a serving plate.
5. Combine olive oil, lime juice, orange juice, and salt in a small basin. Pour the mixture over the salad.
6. Add mint leaves as a garnish and serve right away.

NUTRITION: Calories: 296; Fat: 11g; Protein: 7; Carbs: 49g

31. Whole Wheat Griddle Cakes With Blueberry Orange Compote

Prep time:
10minutes Cook:
15minutes
Servings: 2
Temperature: High

Ingredients:

PANCAKES

- 3/4 heaping cup whole-wheat pastry flour (or sub half whole wheat and half all purpose flour)
- 1/2 cup oats (quick cooking or old fashioned)
- 1 cup well-shaken buttermilk (or 1 cup milk + 1 Tbsp.. lemon juice or vinegar)
- 2 Tbsp. butter (melted)
- 1 large egg (slightly beaten)
- 1 Tbsp. sugar
- 1 pinch salt
- 1 tsp baking powder
- 1/2 tsp baking soda

COMPOTE:

- 1/2 cup blueberries (I used frozen)
- 1 medium orange (zested)
- 2 Tbsp. orange juice
- 1 tsp sugar

Directions:

1. Set a small pot on the stovetop and preheat the griddle to medium heat.
2. In a big bowl, whisk the dry ingredients together. Separately combine the wet ingredients, and then combine the two, stirring just enough to incorporate.
3. Place scant 1/4 cup amounts onto the griddle that has been lightly greased, and heat until bubbles form on top and the sides start to look slightly dry.
4. Turnover and cook for a further 1-2 minutes or until the underside is golden brown.
5. Serve warm with maple and orange-blueberry compote.

NUTRITION: Calories: 491; Fat: 16g; Protein: 14; Carbs: 70g

32.   Grilled Turkey & Havarti Sandwiches

Prep time: 5minutes
Cook: 8minutes
Servings: 1
Temperature: Medium

Ingredients:

- ➢ 3 slices oven-roasted deli turkey
- ➢ 2 slices sourdough bread
- ➢ 2 Tablespoons pesto
- ➢ 1 small tomato, sliced
- ➢ 1 1/2 slices Havarti cheese
- ➢ 2 Tablespoons butter softened

Directions:

1. Put pesto on both slices of bread's interior.
2. Place tomato slices on top of the Havarti cheese slices on one side. (Tip: To prevent soggy bread, place a "barrier" of cheese between the tomatoes and the bread.)
3. Add turkey on top, and then assemble the sandwich.
4. Butter both pieces of bread's exterior before placing them on a hot griddle or in a skillet.
5. Grill the meat until it is toasted and browned on both sides (approximately 3-4 minutes each side)
6. Divide in half and serve warm.

NUTRITION: Calories: 950; Fat: 57g; Protein: 36g; Carbs: 78g

33.   Griddle Cloud Eggs

Prep time: 5minutes
Cook: 4minutes
Servings: 1
Temperature: Low

Ingredients:

- ➢ Egg, large 1 each
- ➢ Parmesan Cheese 1/2 teaspoon

Directions:

1. Set the griddle to the lowest temperature. Do not employ any wind barriers.
2. Divide the egg yolks and whites into different bowls.
3. Whip the egg white for 90 seconds with a hand mixer until a firm peak emerges. Avoid over mixing.
4. Place a parchment paper sheet on the flat top of a heated griddle.
5. Mound the entire amount of fluffy egg white on the parchment paper.
6. Create a small hole in the middle of the whites to resemble a nest.
7. Top the white with a sprinkle of parmesan cheese and spice.
8. Cook for two minutes while covered with a dome.
9. Uncover the egg yolk and place it in the center of the airy egg white.
10. Return the lid and continue cooking for a further two minutes, or until the whites are 11. The yolk is set and is just beginning to turn golden brown.
11. Transfer the cloud egg to a serving plate using a spatula.

NUTRITION: Calories: 75; Fat: 5g; Protein: 7g; Carbs: 0g

34.   Blackstone Fried Rice Recipes

Prep time: 15minutes
Cook: 25minutes
Servings: 1
Temperature: Medium

Ingredients:

- ➤ 4 tablespoons canola oil, divided
- ➤ 1 small onion, diced
- ➤ 1 teaspoon minced garlic
- ➤ 2 duck breasts, diced
- ➤ 1 cup frozen peas and carrots
- ➤ 3 cups cooked Jasmine rice, chilled
- ➤ 2 eggs, lightly beaten
- ➤ 1/8 cup soy sauce
- ➤ 1 teaspoon sesame oil
- ➤ salt and pepper

Directions:

1. Put roughly a tablespoon of oil down on the griddle and heat it to medium-high or high heat.
2. Stir-fry the carrots, frozen peas, and onions until heated through and the edges start to become a bit crispy.
3. Cook the duck breast for 2 to 3 minutes after adding it.
4. Place the duck breast and the vegetables on the griddle's side away from the hot spot.
5. More oil should be added to the griddle, and it should be heated up. The chilled rice should be added and broken up with a spatula. In the final minute of cooking, add the garlic. (Add additional oil as necessary during the procedure.)
6. Combine the rice, veggies, and duck breast: swirl and toss to blend everything. The soy sauce and sesame oil should be uniformly dispersed by the time you drizzle them on top and keep stirring and cooking.
7. Poke a hole in the rice's center, then drizzle with a little extra oil. Using a spatula, mix the eggs inside before tossing them with the rice.

NUTRITION: Calories: 198g; Fat: 10g; Carbs: 13g; Protein: 13g

35. Blackstone Fried Rice Recipes

Prep time: 15minutes
Cook: 25minutes
Servings: 1
Temperature: Medium

Ingredients:

- ➢ 3 pounds ground waygu beef
- ➢ salt and pepper
- ➢ 12 pieces Kurobuta bacon
- ➢ 1 1/2 cups crumbled blue cheese
- ➢ 6 brioche buns
- ➢ toppings of your choosing

Directions:

1. Heat your griddle over medium heat for 10 to 15 minutes.
2. Form your burger into six patties that are slightly larger than your buns and have a depression in the middle while the griddle is heating up.
3. Add salt and pepper to the patties' top and bottom surfaces.
4. Toast your buns and cook the bacon. If your griddle is large enough, you can begin cooking the burgers after the bacon has cooked for about halfway.
5. To achieve medium or medium-rare, the burgers should be cooked for at least 4-5 minutes on each side.
6. Add the blue cheese crumbles to the burgers during the final 3 minutes of cooking, then top with a big dome to let the cheese melt.
7. Assemble, top with your preferred dipping sauce, and enjoy!

NUTRITION: Calories: 1174g; Fat: 76g; Carbs: 34g; Protein: 82g

36.   Bacon Blue Cheese Burgers

Prep time: 5minutes
Cook: 10minutes
Servings: 1
Temperature: Medium

Ingredients:

- ➢ 3 pounds ground beef
- ➢ salt and pepper
- ➢ 8 slices cheese
- ➢ 8 hamburger buns
- ➢ 16 slices bacon

Directions:

1. Make 8 balls of equal size from the hamburgers. Salt and pepper the tops as desired.
2. Heat your flat top, cast iron, or griddle to medium-high to high heat.
3. After placing the burger balls on the grill, use a heavy-duty spatula, bacon press, or burger smasher to quickly smash them down.
4. Season the burger's raw side, then cook it for a few minutes more until a dark-brown crust forms.
5. Sprinkle cheese on top, cover with a melted lid (if required), and cook for a further two minutes or so, or until the bottom has developed a crust.
6. Take the flat top off and serve the food hot!

NUTRITION: Calories: 812; Fat: 49g; Carbss: 24g; Protein:65g

37.   Smash Burgers

Prep time: 10minutes
Cook: 8minutes
Servings: 6
Temperature: Medium

Ingredients:

- 6 Boneless Pork Chops
- 2 eggs
- 3 Tbsp. water
- 3 Tbsp. Butter
- 1 1/2 cups Panko bread crumbs
- 1/2 Grated Parmesan cheese
- 2 Tbsp. fresh parsley chopped
- 1/2 tsp garlic salt
- 1/2 tsp paprika

Directions:

1. Combine the eggs and water in a small bowl. Set aside. Combine the Panko bread crumbs, parmesan cheese, parsley, garlic salt, and pepper in a separate small bowl.
2. Place each pork chop in the bread crumb mixture after dipping it in the egg mixture. Make sure the pork chops are well covered in the coating.
3. Set the Blackstone Grill on medium heat and preheat it (approximately 350 degrees F). Apply butter on the grill and distribute it all over with a spatula.
4. Place the pork chops over the butter on the grill. Cook the pork chops for 2-4 minutes on each side, or until the internal temperature reaches 145 degrees F and the coating is just beginning to become golden.
5. After taking the pork chops off the grill, give them five minutes to rest. They are then prepared for slicing, serving, and enjoying!

NUTRITION: Calories: 339kCal; Fat: 17g; Carbs: 11g; Protein: 33g

38. Blackstone Parmesan Crusted Pork Chops

Prep time: 10minutes
Cook time: 5minutes
Servings: 4
Temperature: medium

Ingredients:

- 3 Large Zucchinis
- 2 Tablespoons Butter
- 2 teaspoons Minced Garlic
- 1 teaspoon Salt
- ½ teaspoon Black Pepper
- 2 Tablespoons Fresh Parmesan Cheese shredded
- 2 teaspoons Fresh Parsley chopped

Directions:

1. Use a spiralizer to cut the zucchini into noodles.
2. Warm the Blackstone Grill to a medium-high temperature (approximately 400 degrees F).
3. Spread the butter out and melt it on the griddle. Add the zucchini noodles and minced garlic to the grill. Stir with tongs and cook the zucchini for 3 to 5 minutes, or until it is soft.
4. Take it off the grill. Add salt and pepper to taste.
5. Serve right away and sprinkle with freshly grated parmesan cheese to enjoy!

NUTRITION: Calories: 89kCal; Carbs: 6g; Protein: 3g; Fat: 7g

39. Blackstone Zucchini Noodles

Prep time: 1hr 15minutes
Cook time: 8minutes
Servings: 6
Temperature: Low

Ingredients:

- ➢ 2 pounds ground beef
- ➢ 1 cup breadcrumbs
- ➢ 1/2 cup Grated Parmesan Cheese
- ➢ 1/4 teaspoon Garlic Powder
- ➢ 1 teaspoon Italian Seasoning
- ➢ 1 teaspoon salt
- ➢ 1 teaspoon pepper
- ➢ 1 Tablespoon Oil

Directions:

1. In a big bowl, combine the meat, breadcrumbs, Parmesan cheese, minced garlic, Italian seasoning, salt, and pepper. Use your hands to blend the ingredients.
2. Shape meatballs into 1 or 2 inch balls. About 24 meatballs should be produced using the recipe. Before frying the meatballs on the griddle, place them in the refrigerator for at least an hour.
3. Add about 1 tablespoon of oil to the Blackstone grill and preheat it over low heat. After the meatballs are brown and beginning to release from the grill, place the meatballs on the grill and let them cook there (3-4 minutes).
4. After the meatballs have been flipped, sauté those until the other side begins to brown (3-4 more minutes).
5. Cook and flip the meatballs continuously until they are internally 165 degrees Fahrenheit.
6. Take the meatballs off the grill and place them on a different platter. Let the meatballs five to ten minutes to sit, then dish out your preferred sauce over spaghetti and savor!

NUTRITION: Calories: 513kCal; Carbs: 15g; Protein: 31g; Fat: 36g

40.   Blackstone Hobo Dinner

Prep time: 15minutes
Cook time: 35minutes
Servings: 4
Temperature: Medium

Ingredients:

- ➢ 1 pound Lean Ground Beef
- ➢ ½ Onion sliced
- ➢ 1 cup Frozen Green beans
- ➢ 3 Carrots peeled and sliced into ¼ inch thick slices
- ➢ 4 Small Russet Potatoes peeled and sliced into ¼ inch thick slices
- ➢ 4 Tablespoons Butter
- ➢ 1 teaspoon Salt
- ➢ 1 teaspoon Pepper

Directions:

1. Turn the Blackstone grill's heat to medium-high (approximately 400 degrees F).
2. Create four equal side patties from the ground meat.
3. Have four large pieces of foil ready and coat them with nonstick cooking spray.
4. Arrange on each piece of oil the sliced potatoes, onions, froz.en green beans, and carrots.
5. Place a beef Pattie on top, sprinkle salt and pepper on each packet, then top each with a tablespoon of butter.
6. To create a packet, fold the foil's sides up.
7. Simply put the foil packages on the grill. The beef should be cooked to an internal temperature of 165 degrees Fahrenheit and the vegetables should be tender, about 35 to 40 minutes into the cooking process (flipping the packets halfway through).
8. Enjoy the food right out of the foil packet!

NUTRITION: Calories: 370kCal; Carbs: 6g; Protein: 22g; Fat: 29g.

41.   Blackstone Popcorn

Prep time: 10minutes
Cook time: 5minutes
Servings: 10
Temperature: High

Ingredients:

- ➤ 2/3 cup Popcorn Kernels
- ➤ 1 Tablespoon Oil
- ➤ 2 Tablespoons Butter
- ➤ 2 teaspoons Salt

Directions:

1. Turn on the Blackstone Grill and heat it up (approximately 500 degrees F). Popcorn can only be made on a hot grill.
2. Put the butter on one side of the grill after putting it in a small saucepan.
3. Put the kernels of popcorn in a small mixing dish. Stir in the first half of the oil to evenly coat the kernels.
4. Use a spatula to spread the remaining oil around the Blackstone grill.
5. After spreading the popcorn kernels evenly around the grill, top it off with a dome. To prevent the popcorn and kernels from burning, continuously move the dome.
6. Cook the popcorn for an additional 2 to 3 minutes, or until all the kernels have popped. When the popping of the kernels stops, the popcorn is finished.
7. Transfer the popcorn from the grill to another bowl using a spatula. Add salt to the top and then drizzle on the melted grill butter.
8. Serve immediately while warm and enjoy!

NUTRITION: Calories: 73kCal; Carbs: 8g; Protein: 1g; Fat: 4g

42.   Sauté Mushrooms and Onions on Blackstone

Prep time: 10minutes
Cook time: 6minutes
Servings: 4
Temperature: Medium

Ingredients:

- ➢ 1 pound Fresh Mushrooms
- ➢ 1 White Onion
- ➢ 2 Tbsp. Avocado Oil
- ➢ 2 Tbsp. Butter
- ➢ 1/2 tsp Salt
- ➢ 1/2 tsp Pepper

Directions:

1. After thoroughly cleaning them, cut the mushrooms into thick slices that are generally 1/2 to 3/8 inch thick. Slice the onion into half-moon that are 3/8 to 2 inches thick.

2. Turn the Blackstone grill's heat to medium-high (approximately 450 degrees F). Then, coat the grill with the butter and avocado oil (or other type of oil). Add the sliced onions and mushrooms on the grill once the butter has melted.

3. Add salt and pepper to them to season them.

4. Cook the mushrooms and onions on the griddle for two to three minutes without stirring.

5. After that, give the mushrooms a gentle shake and cook for a further 2-3 minutes, or until they are lightly browned on both sides.

6. Continue grilling the mushrooms and onions until you get the desired level of tenderness (2-3 more minutes).

7. Take it off the griddle and put it over steak, chicken, or hamburgers. Enjoy!

NUTRITION: Calories: 149kCal; Carbs: 6g; Protein: 4g; Fat: 13g

43. Blackstone Cheeseburger

Prep time: 10minutes
Cook time: 8minutes
Servings: 6
Temperature: Medium

Ingredients:

- ➢ 2 pounds of Ground Beef
- ➢ 1 Tablespoon Oil
- ➢ 1/2 tsp Garlic Salt
- ➢ 1/2 tsp Pepper
- ➢ 6 slices Sharp Cheddar Cheese we used a white cheddar but any will work
- ➢ 6 Hamburger Buns

Directions:

1. Turn the Blackstone Grill's heat to medium-high (approximately 400 degrees F).
2. Use a spatula to spread the oil across the grill.
3. Make six equal balls out of the ground beef, weighing about a third of a pound each.
4. Stand the ground beef on the oil-covered Blackstone grill.
5. Into the Blackstone Grill, firmly press the ground beef balls. To produce a burger patty, press it slightly rather than completely.
6. Use the garlic salt and pepper to season the beef.
7. Fry the patties for three to five minutes.
8. Flip the burgers and continue cooking them until they are fully done (3-4 more minutes).
9. Sprinkle some cheese on top of each hamburger patty.
10. Take out the steak and place it on a hamburger bun.
11. Then enjoy your burger with your favorite toppings!

NUTRITION: Calories: 639kCal; Carbs: 22g; Protein: 37g; Fat: 44g

44.   Blackstone Ribeye Steak

Prep Time: 10minutes
Cook Time: 6minutes
Servings: 4
Temperature: High

Ingredients:

- 4 Ribeye Steaks
- 2 tsp Salt
- 1 tsp Pepper
- 1 tsp Garlic Powder
- 2 Tbsp. Oil
- 2 Tbsp; Butter

Directions:

1. Set the Blackstone griddle to high heat for preheating (approximately 500 degrees F).
1. For the steaks to obtain a decent sear, the griddle needs to be hot.
2. Verify that the steaks are at room temperature and are dry. In a small bowl, mix the salt, pepper, and garlic powder. After that, season the steaks with the seasoning mixture, using about a half teaspoon each steak.
3. Distribute the oil across the Blackstone grill.
4. As soon as the oil is ready, put the steaks on the Blackstone grill on top of the hot oil.
5. To get a decent sear on the steaks, let them cook for two to three minutes without moving them.
6. Turn the steaks over onto a different part of the grill. The steaks should then be cooked for a further 2 to 3 minutes to sear the other side.
7. Next, lower the Blackstone grill's heat setting to medium. The steak should be cooked to your satisfaction.
8. After that, place a small amount of butter on top of each steak and let it to melt into the meat.
9. After 5 minutes of resting, the steak is ready to be served warm and eaten.

NUTRITION: Calories: 586kCal; Carbs: 1g; Protein: 46g; Fat: 45g

45. Turkey Cutlets

Prep time: 5minutes
Cook time: 6minutes
Servings: 1
Temperature: Low

Ingredients:

- Turkey Breast Cutlets. 2 lbs.
- Breadcrumbs, Dry 1 cup
- Parmesan Cheese, Grated 1/4 cup
- Italian Seasoning 1 teaspoon
- Flour, All Purpose 3/4 cup
- Milk 3/4 cup
- Salt 1/2 teaspoon
- Pepper 1/8 teaspoon
- Olive Oil 2 tablespoons

Directions:

1. Make cutlets out of the turkey breasts. Find out how to cut a cutlet of turkey.
2. Turn the Blackstone Griddle to medium-low heat.
3. Set up a dredging station with three components: milk, seasoned flour, and breadcrumb mixture.
4. Begin by coating the turkey cutlet completely with flour.
5. Next, submerge the cutlets in the milk.
6. To make a nice breading, roll the turkey breasts in the breadcrumb mixture.
7. Spread a thin coating of olive oil (or other cooking oil of your choice) across the flat surface of a hot griddle.
8. Place the breaded turkey breast cutlets on the greased griddle, spacing them apart from one another.
9. Depending on the type of griddle and the type of wind that blows around the griddle, cooking times will differ.

NUTRITION: Calories: 318kCal; Carbs: 20g; Protein: 39g; Fat: 8g

46.   Blackstone Potatoes

Prep time: 10minutes
Cook time: 20minutes
Servings: 6
Temperature: medium

Ingredients:

- ➤ 1.5(lbs. Baby Potatoes quartered)
- ➤ 2 Tbsp. Avocado Oil
- ➤ 1 tsp Garlic Powder
- ➤ 1/2 tsp Dried Rosemary
- ➤ 1 tsp Salt
- ➤ 1/2 tsp Pepper

Directions:

1. Turn the Blackstone Grill's heat to medium-high (approximately 400 degrees F.).
2. Combine all the ingredients in a sizable mixing basin. Toss the potatoes to evenly spread the oil and seasonings.
3. Place the potatoes on the grill and cook them until they are cook, about 15-20 minutes, tossing regularly.
4. Immediately serve while still warm and savor!

NUTRITION: Calories: 131kCal; Carbs: 20g; Protein: 2g; Fat: 5g

47. Salmon on Blackstone Griddle

Prep Time: 5minutes
Cook Time: 7minutes
Servings: 3
Temperature: Medium

Ingredients:

- ➢ 1 pound salmon
- ➢ ¼ cup paleo teriyaki sauce
- ➢ 1 tbsp. avocado oil

Directions:

1. First, make 5 to 6 ounce filets of salmon.
2. Next, look for pin bones in your salmon filets. If any, get rid of them. If they are very difficult, try using tweezers or even pliers (make sure you only use kitchen-specific pliers).
3. After that, heat your Blackstone griddle to between 375 and 400F. On my sCale, this is roughly medium high.
4. After the flat top grill has heated up, add the oil.
5. After that, add the salmon filets and cook for 3 minutes with the skin side down.
6. Do a second flip and cook for 2 minutes with the flesh side down.
7. Reverse the salmon to its skin-side-up position and top with teriyaki sauce. Let the salmon to cook for 1-2 minutes, or until it reaches an internal temperature of 145°F and the sauce thickens.
8. Remove from griddle and serve.

NUTRITION: Calories: 277kca; Carbs: 4g; Protein: 31; Fat: 14g

48.   Grilled Shrimp on Blackstone

Prep time: 10minutes
Cook time: 5minutes
Servings: 4
Temperature:

Ingredients:

➢ 16 of Raw Shrimp peeled and deveined

➢ 4 Tbsp. Butter

➢ 1 Tbsp. Minced Garlic

➢ 1/4 tsp Salt

➢ 1/4 tsp Pepper

➢ 1 Lemon juiced

Directions:

1. Bring the Blackstone Griddle's temperature up to medium-high (350-400 degrees F).
1. On the griddle, melt about 1 Tbsp. of the butter. After that, immediately add the shrimp on the griddle with the melted butter.
2. Sauté the shrimp for 2 to 3 minutes on each side, or until pink (only flip the shrimp once).
3. Make a hole in the center of the shrimp on the griddle by moving it. In this space on the griddle, add the remaining butter, minced garlic, salt, and pepper. When the garlic is fragrant, add the shrimp and stir for 1 minute.
4. Take the shrimp off the grill, drizzle some lemon juice on top, and serve.

NUTRITION: Calories: 195kCal; Carbs: 5;, Protein: 16g; Fat: 13g

49. Potato Pancake

Prep time: 5minutes
Cook time: 5minutes
Servings: 8
Temperature: Medium

Ingredients:

- 1½ cups shredded potato
- ¼ cup flour
- 2 eggs
- ¼ cup milk
- ¼ cup finely diced onion
- ¼ cup finely diced green onions
- 1 teaspoon baking powder
- 1 teaspoon salt
- 1 teaspoon pepper

Directions:

1. Whip milk and eggs until foamy.
2. Stir the other ingredients into the egg mixture.
3. Let the mixture sit for 20 minutes.
4. Heat the griddle to medium-high.
5. Skim coat the frying surface with oil, and 6.Add about 14 cup of potato pancake batter when the oil starts to shimmer.
6. Continue with the remaining batter.
7. Flatten the batter and cook each side for 3-4 minutes, flipping once, until golden brown.

NUTRITION: Calories: 90kCal; Carbs: 16g; Protein: 4g; Fat: 1g

50. Wagyu Smash Burger

Prep time: 10minutes
Cook time: 10min
Servings: 5
Temperature: Medium

Ingredients:

- ➢ 1 pound ground beef
- ➢ 4 Burger buns
- ➢ 1 cup Beef Chili
- ➢ 4 sharp cheddar cheese finely grated

Directions:

1. Heat your griddle to 500°F.
2. Cut the meat into four sections of the same size.
3. Stand the meatballs on the griddle.
4. Give the meatball 90 seconds to cook.
5. Cover the beef ball with a square of parchment paper.
6. Use a firm spatula, burger press, or bacon press to press or smash the beef into the griddle.
7. Let the smashed beef to cook for around 90 seconds, or until fluids begin to pool on the flesh.
8. Using a firm spatula, flip the burger over.
9. Give the burger 90 more seconds to fry.
10. If needed, apply more seasoning.
11. Top each hamburger with one of cheddar cheese.
12. Add 14-cup chili to the top of each burger.
13. Serve right away.

NUTRITION: Calories: 522kCal; Carbs: 22g; Protein: 31g; Fat: 34g

51.   French toast Recipe

Prep Time: 5minutes
Cook Time: 8minutes
Serving: 5
Temperature: Medium

Ingredients:

- ➤ 2 Eggs
- ➤ ¼ cup Half and half or milk
- ➤ 1 tablespoon Ground cinnamon
- ➤ 1 loaf French bread
- ➤ 8 strips bacon

Directions:

1. Place the bacon strips on the griddle and start cooking them at 350F in step one.
2. Prepare the other ingredients while the bacon is cooking.
3. Slice the bread into 2 inch thick, thick slices.
4. Add eggs and half-and-half to a large bowl.
5. Add cinnamon to the eggs and incorporate by whisking.
6. Turn the bacon over and transfer it to the other side of the griddle.
7. Dip the French bread slices in the egg mixture, coating both sides for a split second.
8. Cook the egg-dipped bread in rendered bacon grease.
9. Repeat with the remaining slices of bread.
10. After cooking the bacon to the appropriate doneness, remove it and use paper towels to pat it dry.
11. Fry the bread's second side for an additional three minutes, or until golden.
12. Remove the French toast and place two slices of bacon between them.
13. Serve right away

NUTRITION: Calories: 343kCal; Carbs: 58g; Protein: 15g; Fat: 6g

52.   Spicy-Sweet Street Corn

Prep Time: 5minutes
Cook Time:
25minutes Servings:
Temperature: Medium

Ingredients:

- ➤ 4 ears fresh corn
- ➤ 4 slices thick-cut bacon
- ➤ 1 medium sweet onion diced
- ➤ ½ cup pickled jalapeno
- ➤ Optional toppings:
- ➤ Juice of ½ lime
- ➤ ½ cup Cojtilla cheese
- ➤ 1 tablespoon Tajín Clásico Seasoning

Directions:

1. Shuck the corn.
2. Use a sharp knife and the two-bowl method to cut the corn kernels from the cob, being careful to ensure that all the silk has been removed.
3. Put the bacon slices on top of one another.
4. Cut the bacon into dice by first slicing it down the middle.
5. Cut up a sweet onion and cut the jalapeno rings into small pieces by roughly chopping them.
6. Set your Blackstone Griddle for two-zone cooking and preheat it to medium-high.
7. First, fry the bacon until it is about 80% done.
8. Transfer the bacon to the griddle's cool side.
9. Sauté the onion for three minutes in the bacon oil.
10. Include the jalapenos with the onion and cook for three more minutes.
11. Transfer the jalapeño and onion to the griddle's cool side.
12. Sauté the corn for two minutes on the warm side of the griddle while tossing continuously.
13. The corn should be sautéed for around five minutes before being combined with the bacon, onions, and jalapenos.
14. Continue cooking for a further two to three minutes to meld the flavors.
15. Serve in a bowl and, if desired, top with Tajin Classic Seasoning, lime juice, and Costilla cheese.

NUTRITION: Calories: 265kCal; Carbs: 34g; Protein: 11g; Fat: 11g

53. Shrimp Burger on the Blackstone Griddle with Jasmine Rice Bun

Prep Time: 10minutes
Cook Time: 25minutes
Serving: 4
Temperature: Medium

Ingredients:

- Shrimp
- 1 pound raw shrimp peeled and deveined
- 2 tablespoons minced garlic
- 2 tablespoons oil
- 1 tablespoon smoked paprika
- Jasmine Rice Bun
- 4 cups cooked Jasmine rice
- 1 egg
- ½ cup mayonnaise

Other ingredients

- 8 slices bacon
- 1 avocado sliced
- 1 Roma tomato sliced
- Salt and Pepper
- Oil

Directions:

1. Use cooked and cooled jasmine rice to make the buns. Mix the egg, mayonnaise, and rice thoroughly after thoroughly beating the mixture.
2. One cup of rice is pressed into a big ramekin after being covered in plastic wrap. Remove the rice bun with care, and set it on a platter covered with parchment paper.
3. Freeze the rice buns for an hour to make them more durable.
4. Combine the shrimp, oil, paprika, and minced garlic in a sizable mixing dish. Place aside in the fridge for a short marinating period.
5. Turn the griddle's heat up to medium-high and begin cooking the bacon.
6. When the bacon is around halfway done, oil the griddle's open area and add the mostly frozen rice buns.
7. Cook the second side of the bun for three to five minutes, or until it is thoroughly warmed and has a good golden exterior. Set aside.

8. Cook the bacon through and set aside once finished.
9. Before starting to fry the shrimp, distribute any oils or bacon Fat on the griddle into a thin layer using a spatula.
10. Sauté the shrimp for five to seven minutes, or until they are opaque and cooked through.
11. Place the jasmine rice bun on a platter and construct the Shrimp Burger on the Blackstone Griddle dish.
12. Top with bacon, avocado slices, and Roma tomatoes. The shrimp are divided and piled on top.
13. Serve open-faced.

NUTRITION: Calories: 869kCal; Carbs: 70g; Protein: 33g; Fat: 50g

54. Cinnamon French toast

Prep time: 5minutes
Cook time: 10minutes
Servings: 8
Temperature: Medium

Ingredients:

- ➢ 4 large eggs
- ➢ 2/3 cup milk
- ➢ 1/4 cup all-purpose flour
- ➢ 1/4 cup granulated sugar
- ➢ 1/4 teaspoon salt
- ➢ 1 teaspoon ground cinnamon
- ➢ 1 teaspoon vanilla extract
- ➢ 8 thick slices bread

Directions:

1. Heat a skillet over medium heat or the griddle to 350 degrees Fahrenheit.
2. Combine all the ingredients, excluding the bread, in a blender or shallow dish by whisking them all together. Flour and eggs should be combined first, then the following ingredients should be added if whisking by hand.
3. Place bread slices on a hot, oiled griddle or skillet after dipping them into the batter and dredging them thoroughly on both sides.
4. Fry the loaves for a few minutes, or until the bottoms begin to become golden brown. Turn the food over, then continue cooking it there. Take out onto a platter.
5. Warm up before serving with syrup and a dusting of powdered sugar.

NUTRITION: Calories: 89kCal; Carbs: 11g; Protein: 4g; Fat: 3g

55.   Classic Blackstone Pancakes

Prep Time: 5minutes
Cook Time: 15minutes
Servings: 8
Temperature: medium

Ingredients:

- 1 1/2 cups of all-purpose flour
- 3 1/2 tsp of baking powder
- 1 tsp of salt
- 1 tbsp. of white sugar
- 1 1/4 cups of milk
- 1 egg
- 3 tbsp. of butter, melted

Directions:

1. Combine all dry ingredients.
2. Combine all of the wet ingredients, and then add them to the dry components. Gently stir everything together. You should give your griddle 15 minutes to heat up.
3. Do the temperature tests mentioned above to check that your griddle is correctly preheated now that you have your pancake batter ready.
4. Add 1-2 teaspoons of butter or oil to the griddle to grease it.
5. For each pancake, pour roughly 1/4 cup of batter onto the hot griddle. Make sure there is enough room between each pancake so the batter may spread.
6. Observe the pancakes. It is difficult to specify a precise time for cooking pancakes, but flip them over once the top has many bubbles and the slides are slightly brown.
7. After another 2 minutes of cooking, turn off the heat, serve and enjoy.

NUTRITION: Calories: 208kCal; Carbs: 25g; Protein: 5g; Fat: 10g

56.   Blackstone Green Beans

Prep time: 10minutes
Cook time: 10minutes
Servings: 4
Temperature: Medium

Ingredients:

- ➢ Lb. Fresh Green Beans washed and trimmed
- ➢ 1 Tbsp..Avocado Oil
- ➢ 1/2 tsp Garlic Salt
- ➢ 1/4 tsp Pepper

Directions:

1. Prepare your Blackstone griddle over medium high heat (about 400 degrees F) (approximately 400 degrees F).
2. Pour the oil onto the griddle with your spatula. Place the green beans in a single layer on the griddle over the oil. Add some garlic salt and pepper to season them.
3. Sauté the green beans for 7 to 10 minutes, or until they are thoroughly cooked. While you want a little amount of char on the green beans since it gives them plenty of flavor, stir often to prevent scorching.
4. Warm up the food and enjoy!

NUTRITION: Calories: 66kCal; Protein: 2g; Fat: 4g; Carbs: 8g

57. Olive Garden's Herb Grilled Salmon

Prep time: 15minutes
Cook time: 15minutes
Servings: 4
Temperature: Medium

Ingredients:

For the Salmon:

- 4 Salmon Filets with the skin on
- 4 tsp Olive Oil
- 1 Lemon
- 1 Tbsp. Italian Seasoning
- 1 tsp Salt
- 1/2 tsp Pepper

For the Garlic Herb Butter:

- 1/2 cup Unsalted Butter softened at room temperature
- 2 tsp Minced Garlic
- 1 tsp Fresh Parsley chopped

Directions:

1. Arrange the salmon fillets on a big plate for the grilled salmon. Apply lemon juice to the salmon fillets' surface and surrounding area. After that, add Italian seasoning, salt, and pepper to the salmon. On both sides of the salmon, thoroughly rub the seasonings in.

2. To prevent the salmon from sticking to the grill, preheat it to 400 degrees Fahrenheit and put some olive oil on the grates. Brush the salmon with oil on both sides and set it gently skin side down on the grill.

3. Cover the pan and cook the salmon for 14 to 20minutes, or until it flakes easily with a fork.

4. For the herb and garlic butter:

5. In a small bowl, combine all the ingredients.

6. Put the garlic on top of the fish and enjoy.

NUTRITION: Calories: 496, Protein: 35g, Fat: 38g, Carbs: 4g

58. Parmesan Grilled Zucchini

Prep time: 10minutes
Cook time: 8minutes
Servings: 6
Temperature: Medium

Ingredients:

- ➢ 3 Large Zucchini cut in half lengthwise
- ➢ 1 Tablespoon Olive Oil
- ➢ ¼ teaspoon Garlic Powder
- ➢ ½ teaspoon Salt
- ➢ 1/2 teaspoon Black Pepper
- ➢ ½ cup Parmesan Cheese shredded

Directions:

1. Put the chopped zucchini in a sizable mixing dish. Sprinkle them with salt, pepper, and garlic powder before adding a drizzle of olive oil. Use your hands to gently mix the zucchini in the oil and seasonings.

2. Heat the grill to a medium-high temperature (approximately 400 degrees F). To prevent the zucchini from sticking to the grill, clean the grates and brush them with oil.

3. Put the zucchini spears over direct heat on the grill. Sauté the zucchini for four to five minutes, or until it begins to slightly brown. Until the zucchini is cooked, flip it over and grill it for a further 3 to 4 minutes on the other side.

4. Put the shredded parmesan cheese on top of the zucchini. Let it stand for a couple of minutes until it melts.

5. Take off the grill. Enjoy warm servings!

NUTRITION: Calories: 425kCal; Fat: 29g; Protein: 25g; Carbs: 21g

59. Blackstone Cheesy Beef Quesadillas

Prep time: 10minutes
Cook time: 10minutes
Servings: 4
Temperature: Medium

Ingredients:

- ➤ 1 pound Ground Beef
- ➤ 1 teaspoon Minced Garlic
- ➤ 1 teaspoon Onion Powder
- ➤ ½ teaspoon Cumin
- ➤ 1 teaspoon Chili Powder
- ➤ ½ teaspoon Salt
- ➤ ½ teaspoon Black Pepper
- ➤ 1 can Tomato Sauce 8 oz.. can
- ➤ 4 Burrito Size Tortillas 10 inch tortillas
- ➤ 4 cups Colby Jack Cheese shredded

Directions:

1. Turn the Blackstone Grill's heat to medium-high (approximately 400 degrees F).
2. On the Blackstone grill, cook the ground beef over medium-high heat until it is no longer pink and has browned.
3. Add the minced garlic and stir, then cook for one minute, or until the garlic is fragrant. Seasonings and tomato sauce are placed on top of the beef. To thoroughly incorporate all the ingredients, stir well. For one-two minutes, heat on medium-high. Move the ground meat to the Blackstone grill is colder side.
4. Position the tortillas over the Blackstone grill. Half the tortillas should be filled with the beef mixture, and each should have 1 cup of shredded cheese on top. Half-fold the tortilla. Cook the quesadilla until the bottom is golden brown (2-3 minutes). Turnover and continue cooking for an additional 2 to 3 minutes or until the cheese is melted on the other side.
5. Remove from the Blackstone Grill. Each quesadilla is divided into four pieces. Enjoy warm servings!

NUTRITION: Calories: 1039kCal; Fat: 71g; Protein: 58g; Carbs: 43g

60. Chick-Fil-A Grilled Chicken Cool Wrap

Prep time: 5minutes
Total time: 5minutes
Servings: 4
Temperature: Medium

Ingredients:

- ➢ 2 Chicken Breasts Grilled
- ➢ 4 Leaf Lettuce Leaves
- ➢ 1 cup Shredded Monterey Jack and Cheddar Cheese
- ➢ 4 Flaxseed Flour Flat Bread

Directions:

1. Slice up the grilled chicken breasts.
2. Spread out 1 of the flatbread pieces. Add some Leaf lettuce, shredded chicken, and sliced chicken to the top.
3. Serve with your preferred sort of dressing and tightly wrap. I enjoy doing this wrap with Avocado Ranch Lime Dressing.

NUTRITION: Calories: 346kCal; Fat: 12g; Protein: 35;: Carbs: 23g

61.   Blackstone Hibachi Noodles

Prep time: 10minutes
Total time: 10minutes
Servings: 6
Temperature: Medium

Ingredients:

- ➢ 1 Pound Lo Mein Noodles
- ➢ 3 Tablespoons Butter
- ➢ 1 Tablespoon Minced Garlic
- ➢ 3 Tablespoons Brown Sugar
- ➢ 3 Tablespoons Soy Sauce
- ➢ ½ teaspoon salt
- ➢ ½ teaspoon Pepper
- ➢ 1 Tablespoon Sesame Oil
- ➢ 1 Tablespoon Sesame Seeds for topping

Directions:

1. Turn the Blackstone Grill's heat up to medium-high (400 degrees F).
2. Prepare the noodles per the directions on the package until they are al dente.
3. Stir the brown sugar, soy sauce, salt, pepper, and sesame oil together thoroughly in a small mixing dish.
4. On the grill, melt the butter. When the garlic is aromatic, add it back in and cook for another 30 to 60 seconds.
5. Add the cooked noodles after that. After adding the sauce to the noodles, toss them to evenly distribute the sauce mixture throughout. For a few minutes, sauté.
6. Take the grilled food off the heat, sprinkle with sesame seeds, and eat.

NUTRITION: Calories: 367kCal; Protein: 8g; Fat: 10g; Carbs: 62g

62. Blackstone Tiktok Ramen Recipe

Prep time: 10minutes
Cook time: 10minutes
Servings: 1
Temperature: Medium

Ingredients:

- ➢ 1 pkg. Instant Ramen Noodle
- ➢ 1 Tablespoon Butter
- ➢ 1 teaspoon Minced Garlic
- ➢ ½ teaspoon Red Pepper Flakes
- ➢ 1 teaspoon Brown Sugar
- ➢ 1 Tablespoon Soy Sauce
- ➢ 1 Egg slightly beaten
- ➢ 1 teaspoon Everything Bagel Seasoning

Directions:

1. Prepare the ramen noodles in accordance with the directions on the package (do not use the spice packet), then drain them.
2. Turn the Blackstone Grill's heat to medium-high (approximately 400 degrees F).
3. In this skillet, melt the butter. Add the red pepper flakes and minced garlic after stirring. The garlic should be aromatic after 1 minute of cooking. The brown sugar and soy sauce are then combined.
4. Place the noodles on the grill and give them a quick toss to cover them with the sauce mixture. Then, noodle the grill so they are to one side.
5. Increase the temperature to high (450 degrees Fahrenheit) and add the beaten egg to the grill's opposite side. Stir the egg until it is set. After that, combine the noodles with the scrambled egg.
6. Take the dish off the stove, top it with everything bagel seasoning, and serve warm.

NUTRITION: Calories: 570kCal; Fat: 29g; Protein: 17g; Carbs: 61g

63. Blackstone Brats Recipe

Prep time: 10minutes
Cook time: 20minutes
Servings: 6
Temperature: High

Ingredients:

- ➢ 6 Bratwursts
- ➢ 1 tablespoon Avocado Oil
- ➢ 6 Bratwurst Buns
- ➢ Sauerkraut optional

Directions:

1. Turn on the Blackstone Grill and heat it up (approximately 400 degrees F).
2. Spread the avocado oil on the griddle with a spatula after drizzling it on. Then switch the grill's one side off. On the side of the grill that is off, place the bratwursts (indirect heat). Cook the bratwurst for 15-20 minutes, turning it once every 5 minutes, or until the internal temperature reaches 160 degrees F.
3. Transfer the bratwursts to the hot side of the grill and brown them for 1 to 2 minutes on each side.
4. To reheat the buns, either microwave them for 30-60 seconds or grill them for 30-60 seconds over indirect heat.
5. Finally, eat the bratwursts with the sauerkraut on top of the bread!

NUTRITION: Calories: 438kCal; Fat: 24g; Protein:16g; Carbs: 37g

64. Blackstone Hibachi Rice Recipe

Prep time: 10minutes
Cook time: 10minutes
Servings: 6
Temperature: Medium

Ingredients:

- ➢ 2 tablespoon butter
- ➢ 4 cups cooked rice cooled
- ➢ 2 tablespoon sesame oil
- ➢ 3 tablespoon soy sauce
- ➢ 1 teaspoon salt
- ➢ 1 teaspoon pepper
- ➢ 3 large eggs light beaten

Directions:

1. Turn on the Blackstone grill and heat it to medium-low (approximately 350 degrees F).
2. Put the butter to the griddle and spread it out with your spatula. After that, add the cooked rice on the griddle and season it with salt, pepper, soy sauce, sesame oil, and more. The rice should be heated through and slightly browned after 3-4 minutes of sautéing on the griddle.
3. Slide the rice to one side of the Blackstone griddle, and then add the beaten eggs.
4. Use the griddle to scramble the eggs.
5. Combine the rice and eggs.
6. Immediately serve warm, and savor!

NUTRITION: Calories: 563kCal; Fat: 11g; Protein: 13g; Carbs: 99g

65. Canned Biscuits On Blackstone

Prep time: 10minutes
Cook time: 15minutes
Servings: 8
Temperature: High

Ingredients:

- ➤ 1 pkg. Biscuits
- ➤ 1 Tbsp. Butter

Directions:

1. Preheat the Blackstone grill over medium heat (approximately 350 degrees F). Watch the grill carefully and make sure that it does not get too hot or the biscuits will burn.
2. Place a wire rack on one side of the grill and spread the butter out on the other side of the grill with a metal spatula.
3. Open the biscuits and place each one directly on the heated grill. Cook for 1-2 minutes until golden brown. Flip and cook the opposite side for 1-2 minutes until golden brown.
4. Move the biscuits onto the wire rack on the griddle and make sure that they are not touching the surface directly or they may burn.
5. Close the griddle cover and cook for 10-15 more minutes until the biscuits are cooked through. Watch the biscuits closely so that they not burn and make sure to keep the griddle on low so that it does not exceed 350 degrees F.
6. Remove from the griddle to a plate. Serve warm, topped with butter and enjoy!

NUTRITION: Calories: 158kCal; Fat: 9g; Protein: 2g; Carbs: 18g

66.   Blackstone Scrambled Eggs

Prep time:
10minutes Cook
time: 15minutes
Servings: 8
Temperature: High

Ingredients:

> 1 egg
> butter or bacon grease

Directions:

1. In a sizable mixing bowl, stir the eggs, milk, salt, and pepper.

2. Warm up the Blackstone griddle on a medium heat (to approximately 350-375 degrees F). Oil the griddle with oil, butter or bacon grease so that the eggs does not stick.

3. Slather the griddle with the egg mixture. Using a large spatula, move the eggs to the center of the griddle as they started to set to create curdled eggs. Continue doing this until all of the eggs are cooked, but they still have a slight wet appearance to prevent drying out.

4. As soon as you remove the eggs from the heat, you can consume them.

NUTRITION: Calories: 172kCal; Fat: 13g; Protein: 11g; Carbs: 1g

67.   Blackstone Italian Dunkers

Prep time: 10minutes
Cook time: 15minutes
Servings: 1
Temperature: Low

Ingredients:

- ➢ 1 loaf Italian (or French) bread
- ➢ 1 stick salted butter
- ➢ 2 tablespoons Johnny's Garlic Bread Seasoning
- ➢ 1 cup shredded Parmesan cheese
- ➢ 2 cups shredded mozzarella cheese (optional, and not included in photos)
- ➢ 1 pound ground beef
- ➢ 1-teaspoon salt, pepper, garlic blend (or approximately 1/3 teaspoon of each to add up to 1 teaspoon if you do not have a blend.)
- ➢ 1 - 48 ounce jar marinara

Directions:

1. Slice the bread into rounds. Combine the butter and Garlic Bread seasoning, and spread over both the front and the back of the cuts.
2. Preheat the Blackstone over low heat. You want to run it around 325°ish for the best results.
3. Cook the ground beef over medium heat. Place the cooked ground beef into a saucepan and top with the marinara sauce. Place the pan on the griddle to heat while you are toasting your garlic bread.
4. Toast each side of the garlic bread until golden brown. If desired, top with cheese(s) and cover or pop into an oven under a broiler for a minute until it is melted and bubbly.
5. Serve the toasted garlic bread with the meaty marinade for dipping!

NUTRITION: Calories: 633kCal; Fat: 43g; Protein: 37g; Carbs: 25g

68.   Griddle Crab Cakes

Prep time: 10minutes
Cook time: 10minutes
Servings: 1
Temperature: Medium

Ingredients:

- ➤ 1 bag Shredded Hash Browns 30 oz. bag
- ➤ 3 Tbsp. Butter
- ➤ 4 crabs

Directions:

1. A box grater must be used to shred fresh butternut squash.
2. Compile all the materials for the crab cakes that will be grilled on the griddle. Crabmeat should be drained of any liquid.
3. Combine the butternut squash freshly shreds, egg, Italian breadcrumbs, crabmeat, salt, and pepper in a medium bowl. By gently folding with a spoon or your hands, combine all ingredients.
4. Create five equal balls from the crab cake mixture. Form a tiny patty by pressing the butternut squash crab cake mixture together. It will take considerable patience and practice to do this. The patties should be between two and three inches wide.
5. The Blackstone flat top griddle was preheated. When the oil is hot, add a thin layer and spread it out evenly with a griddle spatula. Place the crab cake patties gingerly onto the hot, oiled griddle.
6. Use a griddle spatula to gently push the patties onto the griddle and cook them over medium heat.
7. Use a spatula to turn the burger after allowing it to cook for about 4 minutes or until it is golden brown. If necessary, add more oil. The second side should be cooked until golden brown. Your griddle-grilled crab cakes should not be overcooked!
8. When they are still hot, serve right away. Add your preferred dipping sauce, such as pesto aioli or tartar sauce, on top.

NUTRITION: Calories: 147; Fat: 5g; Protein: 10g; Carbs: 6g.

69.   Patty Melt

Prep time: 5minutes
Cook time: 10minutes
Servings: 1
Temperature: Medium

Ingredients:

- ➢ Bread, Thick Cut 2 slices
- ➢ Ground Beef 8 ounces
- ➢ Onion, Sweet White. 1/2 cup
- ➢ Butter 1 Tablespoon
- ➢ Swiss Cheese, Slices 2 each

Directions:

1. Warm up the Blackstone Griddle.
2. The onion should be thinly sliced.
3. Melt 1 tablespoon of the butter on a hot griddle. Sliced onion is placed on top of the heated butter. The onion should be caramelized until it turns a golden brown color.
4. Place two to four ounce hamburger balls on the Blackstone Griddle to cook the crumbled burger patties. Then, using the griddle spatula, crush the meat into extremely thin patties on top of a sheet of parchment paper. Let the patties to fry for 2 to 3 minutes, or until they are golden brown and crispy. The patties should be turned over and crisped up on the other side. To avoid going over, add the cheese before the burger is finished.
5. Toast the bread on the flat top griddle with butter.
6. Assemble the sandwich by placing the toasted side of one piece of bread on the bottom, followed by the cheese burger patties, caramelized onions, and, if preferred, patty melt secret sauce. Using the top piece of bread, complete the patty melt recipe sandwich, making sure the toasted side is out.
7. Offer hot beside your preferred sides.

NUTRITION: Calories: 557Cal; Fat: 35g; Protein: 42g; Carbs: 21g

70.   Pulled Pork Grilled Cheese Sandwich

Prep time: 5minutes
Cook time: 5minutes
Servings: 1
Temperature: Medium

Ingredients:

- Bread, Sliced 2 each
- Cheddar Cheese, Slice 1 each
- Pulled Pork 2 oz..
- Butter 1 Tablespoon
- BBQ Sauce 1 Tablespoon

Directions:

1. Combine all of the ingredients you will need to produce the best grilled cheese sandwich.
2. Every piece of bread should first have one side buttered.
3. Flip one of the pieces of bread over so the butter side is on the bottom and the un-buttered side is facing up.
4. Place a layer of cheddar cheese on top of the bread.
5. After that, cover the cheese with a layer of finely chopped pulled pork.
6. Add a little of your favorite BBQ sauce to the pulled pork for a garnish.
7. The second slice of bread should be placed on top of the BBQ pulled pork with the buttered side facing up. Cook food in a griddle pan for about 2 minutes on each side, or until both sides are brown. If a griddle weight is available, use it.

NUTRITION: Calories: 494; Fat: 25g; Protein: 19;: Carbs: 47g

71. Keto Philly Cheesesteaks

Prep time: 5minutes
Cooking time: 5minutes
Servings: 4
Temperature: Medium

Ingredients:

- Keto Philly Cheesesteaks Recipe Ingredients
- SUPER EASY Keto dinner idea made on the Blackstone Griddle Grill!
- 1 package of Steak-Umms or thinly sliced steak or 4 servings based on the package
- 8 slices Provolone cheese
- 1 green bell pepper
- 1 small yellow onion
- 2 tbsp. olive oil
- Keto Philly Cheesesteak Sauce Topping
- 1 part Dukes Mayonnaise
- 1 part Sriracha sauce
- 4 Keto Hotdog Buns

Directions:

1. Turn the grill's griddle to medium heat. Add the precut veggies and 2 tablespoons of olive oil on one side of the grill (bell pepper and onions).
2. When required, turn the vegetables and steak. The steak will cook the quickest and be done first, so lower the heat on that side of the grill and move it there.
3. Flip the griddle grill's other side to low heat.
4. On each bun, add the meat and vegetable combination with two slices of provolone cheese. To assist the cheese melt more quickly, cover with the cooking cover.
5. Each Philly Cheesesteak should be taken out of the container with the help of the spatula and placed on a serving platter.
6. Just before serving, take the sauce out of the fridge and drizzle it over each Philly cheesesteak.
7. Enjoy warm servings!

NUTRITION: Calories: 379kCal; Fat: 26g; Carbs: 8g; Protein: 31g

72.   Blackstone Kimchi Gyoza

Prep time: 30minutes
Cook time: 15minutes
Servings: 1
Temperature: Low

Ingredients:

- ➢ 1 package round gyoza wrappers
- ➢ 1 pound ground pork
- ➢ 1 cup kimchi, chopped
- ➢ 1 bunch green onions or sCallions (greens only), chopped
- ➢ 1 tablespoon minced garlic
- ➢ 2 teaspoons sesame oil
- ➢ 3 tablespoons soy sauce
- ➢ 1 tablespoon mirin
- ➢ 1/2 teaspoon gochujang (optional)

Directions:

1. In a bowl, mix the ground pork with the kimchi, green onions, garlic, sesame oil, soy sauce, mirin, and gochujang (if using). Using your hands, combine the ingredients until they are all distributed equally.
2. Gently peel one of the wrappers off the packaging, dampening the edges. A heaping tablespoon of filling should be placed inside before being folded in half.
3. Fold the corners of the gyoza inward slightly, then continue the process until all of the filling has been used.
4. Spend 10 to 15 minutes heating up your Blackstone Griddle over low heat. The gyoza should be placed on the oiled griddle seam-side up after being liberally coated with oil.
5. Cook for 3 to 4 minutes, or until golden brown on the bottom.
6. Prepare a large dome-shaped cover, squirt some water onto the griddle in the middle of the dumplings, and rapidly cover to steam. As soon as you hear the water burning off, check the dumplings. At least 160 degrees must be reached inside. Steam a little bit more if it is not.
7. Take out and offer dipping sauce.

NUTRITION: Calories: 195; Protein: 15g; Carbs: 3g; Fat: 13g

73. Vegetable Yakisoba

Prep time: 10minutes
Cooking time: 15minutes
Servings: 1
Temperature: Medium

Directions:

SAUCE

- 2 tablespoons soy sauce
- 4 tablespoons water
- 2 tablespoons mirin
- 1 teaspoon sesame oil
- 2 teaspoons minced garlic
- 2 teaspoons chili garlic sauce

- 1 teaspoon sriracha
- 2 tablespoons brown sugar
- 1/2 teaspoon ground ginger
- 1 tablespoon cornstarch
- 1 teaspoon canola oil

STIR-FRY

- 3-4 tablespoons oil
- 1/2 cup sliced onions
- 1 sliced bell pepper
- 1 cup chopped broccoli

- 1 cup sliced zucchini
- 1/2 cup matchstick carrots
- 1 handful baby spinach (optional)
- 17 ounces fresh yakisoba noodles

Directions:

1. Whisk the sauce components together after adding them all together.
2. Heat your griddle to medium-high heat. Add 1 tablespoon of oil and a dash of sesame oil. Stir-fry the vegetables for a brief period, until they are crisp-tender (about 3-4 minutes).
3. Add the noodles, vegetables, and shrimp to the hot griddle after heating the other tablespoon of oil. Add the sauce after one minute of stirring.
4. Stir until the sauce has thickened, retaining as much of it with the noodles as possible (and avoiding having it run into the oil bucket), and serve right away.

NUTRITION: Calories: 225kCal; Fat: 9g; Carbs: 18g; Protein: 16g

74. Blackstone Crab Scampi

Prep time: 10minutes
Cooking time: 15minutes
Servings: 1
Temperature: Medium

Ingredients:

- 6 pounds pre-cooked crab
- 1 cup melted salted butter
- 2 teaspoons kosher salt
- 1 tablespoon Old Bay seasoning blend
- 2 tablespoons minced garlic
- 1 cup dry white wine

Directions:

1. Set your griddle to medium heat for preheating.
2. Lay the crab on the griddle, season with salt and Old Bay, and coat with the mixture. Garlic should be smeared over, followed by butter. Use the tons to move the crabs and garlic butter around on the griddle during the final minute of cooking.
3. Cover the crab with the wine and steam for two to three minutes.
4. Continue scraping and spooning the wine, garlic, and butter sauce over the top of the crabs with a bench scraper.
5. Remove and warmly serve!

NUTRITION: Calories: 686kCal; Fat: 34g; Carbs: 2g; Protein: 84g

75.   Cupcakes on A Blackstone Griddle

Prep time: 5minutes
Cooking time: 10minutes
Servings: 1
Temperature: Low

Ingredients:

- ➢ Yellow Cake Mix 15.25 oz.
- ➢ Vegetable Oil 1/3 cup
- ➢ Eggs, Large 3 each
- ➢ Water 1 cup

Directions:

1. Assemble all the components needed to make your Blackstone cupcakes.
2. Set your griddle's heat to the lowest level.
3. Following the instructions on the cake mix box, combine the eggs, oil, water, and cake mix in a mixing dish.
4. Be sure to mix for 2 minutes to assist the batter's lumps dissolve. Just make sure not to over-mix the batter.
5. Line your metal muffin pan with paper liners.
6. Use a # 20 scooper to only partially fill the muffin liners.
7. Place the cupcake pan on the heated griddle using the warmed griddle, then immediately cover the entire pan. You can use a basting cover, your hard cover griddle lid, or a disposable foil pan from the dollar shop. By doing so, the griddle's heated heat may be trapped and used to bake the cupcakes.
8. Just be careful not to check on the cupcakes too frequently because that could allow the heat to escape the lid. When evaluating the cupcakes for doneness, give them a slight peak.
9. If you see that the bottoms of the cupcakes are burning, try the trick of placing crumpled foil pieces in the shape of an X on top of the griddle but underneath the cupcake pan.

NUTRITION: Calories: 103kCal; Fat: 4; Carbs: 15g; Protein: 1g

76.   Cinnamon French toast

Prep time: 5minutes
Cooking time: 10minutes
Servings: 1
Temperature: Medium

Ingredients:

➢ Cinnamon Raisin Bread, slices 4 each

➢ Eggs 2 each

➢ Milk 2 tablespoons

➢ Vanilla 1 teaspoon

➢ Cinnamon, Ground 1/4 teaspoon

➢ Butter 2 tablespoons

Directions:

1. Compile all the ingredients you will need to prepare homemade French toast.
2. Combine the eggs, milk, cinnamon, and vanilla in a small bowl. Mix everything with a fork until thoroughly combined.
3. Cut the bakery bread into the required thickness of slices.
4. Set your pan's heat to medium. To cook the French toast, coat a pan with cooking spray or use a small amount of butter.
5. Dip each slice of bread into the egg mixture for a brief period. After turning it over, leave the bread alone for a short while.
6. Gently add the bread that has been egg-covered to the heated pan, and brown it on both sides. To create an even brown hue on my toast, I like to lightly pat the bread with a spatula. TypiCal cooking durations range from one to two minutes per side.
7. After it is finished, put the French toast on a serving platter and keep cooking it until it is all done.
8. Add your preferred topping on top.

NUTRITION: Calories: 336kCal; Fat: 19g; Carbs: 30g; Protein: 11g

77.   Blackstone English Muffins

Prep time: 20minutes
Cooking time: 20minutes
Servings: 1
Temperature: Medium

Ingredients:

- 1 3/4 cups whole milk, lukewarm
- 4 tablespoons salted butter, room temperature
- 1 1/2 teaspoons salt
- 2 1/2 tablespoons sugar
- 1 large egg, lightly beaten
- 4 1/2 cups (539g) Unbleached Bread Flour
- 2 teaspoons instant yeast
- cornmeal for sprinkling

Directions:

1. Fill the mixer with the milk, yeast, butter, egg, sugar, salt, and flour. Stir on low until all ingredients are combined, then increase the speed to medium and continue mixing for about 5 minutes.
2. The dough will be incredibly smooth and elastic when you remove it. Turn the kneaded dough to coat it in oil after placing it in a bowl.
3. Cover the dough and let it to rise until it has roughly doubled in size. More flavor emerges as it rises more slowly.
4. Create slick balls out of the dough. On the surface of your cool Blackstone or into your cold pans, sprinkle some cornmeal.
5. Take your dough balls and flatten them into discs that are about 3/4 inch thick and 2-3 inches across once your griddle or pans are ready.
6. Cook each side for approximately 10 minutes. To ensure they are not over browning, check them after 5 minutes.
7. Place your muffins on a baking sheet and bake them at 350 degrees for 15 minutes if the outside of the muffins are browning too quickly and the interior is not fully cooked.
8. After letting them cool for 10 to 15 minutes, divide them with a fork, and enjoy!

NUTRITION: Calories: 355kCal: Fat: 8g: Carbs: 60g: Protein: 11g

78. Blackstone Raspberry Pancakes

Prep time: 10minutes
Cooking time: 20minutes
Servings: 1
Temperature: Low

Ingredients:

RASPBERRY SYRUP

- ➢ 1-pint raspberries (can be frozen, but fresh is best)
- ➢ 1/2 cup water
- ➢ 1/2 cup sugar
- ➢ 1 teaspoon vanilla
- ➢ juice of 1 lemon
- ➢ 1 teaspoon corn starch
- ➢ 1 tablespoon cold water

PANCAKES

- ➢ 5 eggs
- ➢ 1 1/2 cups milk
- ➢ 1/2 cup butter, melted
- ➢ 5 cups buttermilk
- ➢ 1 TBSP. vanilla

Directions:

1. Mix all of the sauce's ingredients, excluding the cold water and cornstarch. Simmering while being heated on a medium-low heat setting. While you combine the pancake batter, reduce the heat to low and allow the mixture to simmer for 15 to 20 minutes.
2. In a bowl, combine all of the ingredients for the pancakes with the exception of the fresh berries and whisk.
3. Heat your griddle to a low temperature. After it has fully preheated, butter all the areas where a pancake will be placed.
4. Spoon some raspberries on top of a tiny amount of batter that has been placed on the griddle. Cook for a further two to three minutes, or until the bottom is browned.
5. Using a spatula, carefully flip the food and let the other side to cook.
6. Keep frying the pancakes until they are all finished.
7. To complete the raspberry sauce, whisk in a slurry made by combining cold water and cornstarch. Simmer it for a while to thicken.

8. Cover the pancakes with the sauce and serve immediately.

NUTRITION: Calories: 854kCal: Fat: 24g: Carbs: 134g: Protein: 26g

79. Blackened Shrimp Caesar Wrap

Prep time: 10minutes
Cooking time: 10minutes
Servings: 1
Temperature: Medium

Ingredients:

- 1 pound peeled and deveined shrimp
- 1 tablespoon Cajun blackening season
- 1/2 teaspoon salt
- 1/4 teaspoon cayenne pepper
- 1 tablespoon olive oil
- 1 small cucumber
- 1 medium tomato
- 1/2 cup creamy Caesar dressing
- 1 head romaine lettuce
- 4 large tortilla shells
- 1 tablespoon shredded parmesan

Directions:

1. Dice your cucumber and tomato into 1/2" pieces first, and then set them aside. Then, separate your romaine lettuce into pieces that are 1 to 1 1/2" in size.
2. After washing them, dry your shrimp with a paper towel before putting them in a medium-sized bowl.
3. Toss the shrimp in the bowl with the Cajun seasoning, salt, and cayenne pepper until they are all thoroughly coated.
4. After the griddle has reached a medium heat temperature, pour the olive oil onto it and spread it out evenly.
5. Place all the shrimp on the griddle's surface, over the area with the olive oil, and cook for 1 1/2 to 2 minutes.
6. Turn the shrimp over and cook on the other side for an additional 1 1/2 to 2 minutes.
7. After removing the shrimp from the skillet, give them 10 minutes to cool. The tortillas should be heated briefly on the griddle to soften them while the shrimp cool.
8. Start assembling your wraps after the shrimp have cooled.
9. Combine the shrimp with the lettuce, cucumber, and tomato in a big bowl. Add the Caesar dressing and blend by drizzling it on.
10. One of the tortillas should be spread out on a level surface. Add some salad on the tortilla and sprinkle parmesan cheese on top.

11. Be sure to carefully enclose everything, keeping everything inside the tortilla.
12. Enjoy by cutting your wrap in half at a 45-degree angle.

NUTRITION: Calories: 524kCal: Fat: 7g: Carbs: 24g: Protein: 36g

80. Stuffed Breakfast Croissant with Steak

Prep time: 10minutes
Cooking time: 10minutes
Servings: 1
Temperature: Medium

Ingredients:

- ➤ 4 croissants
- ➤ 6 ounces ribeye steak, cooked
- ➤ 2 tablespoons butter
- ➤ 8 large eggs
- ➤ 1/4 cup whole milk
- ➤ 1/4 teaspoon black pepper
- ➤ 1/4 teaspoon garlic salt
- ➤ 4 ounces shredded cheddar cheese

Directions:

1. Set your oven to warm or low and add the croissants.
2. Cut the cooked steak into cubes and set it aside.
3. Over low to medium heat, melt the butter in a medium nonstick skillet or on your Blackstone   griddle.
4. Whip together your eggs, milk, salt, and pepper while the butter is melting.
5. Add the steak to the heated butter and let it sear for a few seconds.
6. Pour the eggs over the melted butter and scramble them softly with a rubber spatula.
7. Flip once, and then include the cheese crumbs.
8. Cook the eggs covered over low heat until they are done and the cheese has melted.
9. Take the croissants out of the oven and cut them in half. The eggs should be stuffed within. Serve warm!

NUTRITION: Calories: 706kCal: Fat: 24g: Carbs: 33g: Protein: 36g

81. Blackstone Air Fryer Lobster Tails

Prep time: 10minutes
Cooking time: 7minutes
Servings: 1
Temperature: Medium

Ingredients:

- ➢ 6 lobster tails, split
- ➢ 1 teaspoon salt
- ➢ 1 teaspoon paprika
- ➢ 1 teaspoon Old Bay
- ➢ 1/2 teaspoon pepper
- ➢ 6 tablespoons smoked garlic butter (or some salted butter with garlic powder also works in a pinch)

Directions:

1. Using kitchen shears or a sharp knife cut the lobster tails in half. The lobster tail can also be butter flyed by slicing through the Centre of the top of the shell, drawing it apart, separating the meat from the shell, and then closing the shell over the meat so it is resting on top.
2. Season the meat with salt, paprika, Old Bay, and pepper after brushing it with garlic butter.
3. Set your air fryer to 450° (or "high" if it only goes up to 450°).
4. Put the lobster tails in and cook them for 5-7 minutes with the meat-side up.
5. Take out, serve hot, and brush with additional garlic butter (if desired).

NUTRITION: Calories: 136kCal: Fat: 2g: Carbss: 6g: Protein: 23g

82. Blackstone Marinated Sautéed Mushrooms

Prep time: 10minutes
Cooking time: 5minutes
Servings: 1
Temperature: Medium

Directions:

- ➤ ounces mushrooms
- ➤ 1 tablespoon red wine vinegar
- ➤ 1/4 teaspoon salt
- ➤ 1/4 teaspoon pepper
- ➤ 2 tablespoons butter

Directions:

1. If required, separate the mushrooms. Pour the red wine vinegar over the top after seasoning with salt and pepper. Stir continuously until the majority of the liquid is absorbed.
2. Heat your Blackstone griddle or cast-iron pan over medium heat. Melt the butter by adding it to the heating pan. Pour the mushrooms onto the frying surface as soon as it has melted.
3. Let the mushrooms simmer for two to three minutes. Stir after removing the cover. Cook covered for an additional 2 to 3 minutes.
4. Remove and warmly serve.

NUTRITION: Calories: 40kCal: Fat: 4g: Carbs: 1g: Protein: 0g

83. Blackstone Hash Browns

Prep time: 10minutes
Cooking time:
10minutes Servings: 6
Temperature: Medium

Ingredients:

- ➢ 1 bag Shredded Hash Browns 30 oz. bag
- ➢ 3 Tbsp. Butter

Directions:

1. Put a medium heat source under the Blackstone griddle (to approximately 350 degrees F). Using the spatula spread the butter across the griddle and let it to melt.
2. Distribute the hash browns into serving sizes on the griddle after placing them there. If the thickness is uniform, tap them down with your spatula. Do not touch them after that. Approximately 6 minutes of cooking (without touching them). To see if they are brown, gently lift one edge. If the hash browns are golden, flip them over and cook them for a further 4-6 minutes until the other side is brown.
3. After that, carefully take them off the grill. Enjoy warm servings!

NUTRITION: Calories: 166kCal: Fats: 7g: Carbs: 25g: Protein: 3g

84.　Blackstone Beef and Broccoli

Prep time: 30minutes
Cooking time:
5minutes Servings: 6
Temperature: Medium

Ingredients:

- ➢ 2 Tablespoons Vegetable Oil
- ➢ 2 pounds Flank Steak thinly sliced
- ➢ 2 Tablespoons Cornstarch
- ➢ 3 Tablespoons Cold Water
- ➢ 2 cups Broccoli chopped into bite size pieces
- ➢ 6 cups White Rice cooked

FOR THE SAUCE:

- ➢ 1 Tablespoon Cornstarch
- ➢ 1 Tablespoon Minced Garlic
- ➢ 3 Tablespoons Brown Sugar
- ➢ 2 Tablespoons Rice Vinegar

Directions:

1. Put the meat in a zip lock bag in step one. In a small bowl, combine the cornstarch and cold water. Include this in the meat bag. For at least 20 to 30 minutes, marinate.
2. Set the Blackstone grill to medium-high heat for preheating. On the grill, spread the vegetable oil. The steak should be placed on the grill, and the chopped broccoli should be placed next to the steak. After the steak is brown and the broccoli is soft, cook the beef and vegetables for 3-4 minutes.
3. In a small bowl, combine all the sauce ingredients. Mix the beef and vegetables together after adding the sauce. To ensure that all the flavors are blended and thoroughly cooked, heat for 1-2 minutes.
4. Take the food off the grill, serve it warm over rice, and savor it!

NUTRITION: Calories: 976kCal: Fat: 13g: Carbs: 160g: Protein: 47g

85.   Blackstone Asparagus with Bacon

Prep time: 10minutes
Cooking time:
10minutes Servings: 6
Temperature: Medium

Ingredients:

➢ 1 lb. Asparagus

➢ 6 Slices Bacon diced

➢ 1 tsp Minced Garlic

➢ 1/2 tsp Salt

➢ 1/4 tsp Pepper

Directions:

1. Trim the rough ends off the asparagus's bottom, and then cut it into quarters.

2. Turn the Blackstone grill's heat to medium-high (approximately 400 degrees F).

3. Grill the diced bacon for 2 to 3 minutes, or until it begins to color.

4. Add the asparagus pieces and mix. Add salt and pepper to taste. Mix all the ingredients together to properly blend them. When the bacon is crispy and the asparagus is tender, sauté for 5-7 minutes. Next add the minced garlic and heat for a further 30 seconds, or until fragrant.

5. Take off the grill. Enjoy while still warm and serve right away!

NUTRITION: Calories: 108kCal: Fat: 9g: Carbs: 4g: Protein: 5g

86.   Lemon Oregano Grilled Chicken Tenders

Prep time: 5minutes
Cooking time:
10minutes Servings: 6
Temperature: Medium

Ingredients:

> Chicken – Look for pre-cut chicken tenders or slice chicken breast into strips using our guide below.

> Lemon - Freshly squeezed lemon juice will give you the most flavor.

> Olive Oil - This recipe can handle the bold flavor of extra virgin olive oil. Otherwise, select a light neutral oil.

> Oregano - This adds an earthy, slightly spicy, slightly sweet flavor

> Salt and pepper - Salt and pepper can really enhance other flavors in food.

Directions:

1. Sliced chicken should be placed in a bag or bowl with the other ingredients for the marinade, and the mixture should be refrigerated for 30 minutes to several hours.

2. Heat a grill or griddle to medium-high heat and oil the grates.

3. The chicken should be grilled for 6 to 8 minutes, turning it over halfway through.

4. Dispense and savor!

NUTRITION: Calories: 224.6kCal: Fat: 10.3g: Carbs: 13.3g: Protein: 31.3g

87. Grilled Buffalo Chicken Flatbread Pizza Recipe

Prep time: 10minutes
Cook time: 10minutes
Servings: 1
Temperature: medium

Ingredients:

- 1 8 oz.. Bag of Diced Chicken Breast, Pre-Cooked
- 2 7.5 oz.. Packages of Naan Flatbread
- 1/2 Cup of Ranch Dressing
- 1/3 Cup of Buffalo Sauce
- 1 16 oz.. Bag of Shredded Mozzarella Cheese
- 1 Bunch of Green Onions, Chopped

Directions:

1. Preheat the grill to between 350 and 375 degrees.
2. Combine the ranch dressing and buffalo sauce in a bowl.
3. Top your flatbread with the buffalo sauce mixture.
4. Add pieces of chicken breast, mozzarella, and green onions on top.
5. Grill the item for 5 to 10 minutes, or until the cheese is melted and bubbling.
6. Take the grill out, then serve right away.

NUTRITION: Calories: 825kCal: Fat: 42g: Protein: 53g: Carbs: 57g.

88. Balsamic Marinade for Grilled Vegetables

Prep time: 5minutes
Cook time: 10minutes
Servings: 6
Temperature: medium

Ingredients:

- 4 tbsp. olive oil
- 2 tbsp. lemon juice
- 2 tbsp. balsamic vinegar
- 1 tbsp. Dijon mustard
- 1 tbsp. honey (or maple syrup, optional)
- 2 garlic cloves, minced
- 1 tsp Italian seasoning
- 1/2 tsp kosher salt (more to taste)
- 1/2 tsp black pepper

Directions:

1. Combine the olive oil, balsamic vinegar, garlic, salt, and pepper in a small bowl. Set aside. Spray cooking spray on the grill and preheat it slowly.
2. Arrange the vegetables on the grill in a single layer, cover them, and cook for 12 minutes, flipping once. The vegetables should have lovely grill marks and be soft to the touch. If you prefer softer vegetables, cook them longer.
3. Add the vegetables to a large bowl, drizzle with balsamic dressing, top with parsley or basil, and toss to combine.
4. Serve with quinoa or brown rice on the side and grilled meat or seafood.

NUTRITION: Calories: 92kCal: Fat: 5g: Protein: 2g: Carbs: 10g

89.   Best Blackstone Chicken Breasts

Prep time: 10minutes
Cook time: 10minutes
Servings: 6
Temperature: Medium

Ingredients:

➢ 3 Chicken Breasts filleted into 6 pieces

➢ 1 Tbsp... Avocado Oil

➢ 1/4 tsp Garlic Powder

➢ 1 tsp Salt

➢ 1/2 tsp Pepper

Directions:

1. Get the grill ready by heating it to medium-high (approximately 400 degrees F).

2. Apply the avocado oil on the griddle and spread it out with your spatula.

3. After that, put the chicken breasts that have been filled on the griddle and season them with salt, pepper, and garlic powder.

4. Let them brown for 4-6 minutes. When the chicken reaches an internal temperature of 165 degrees F, flip it over and cook for another 5-6 minutes.

5. Remove the chicken from the griddle.

6. Give it five minutes to rest.

7. At that point, you can serve and eat it.

NUTRITION: Calories: 150kCal: Fat: 5g: Protein: 24g: Carbs: 1g

90. Griddled Fruit Salad

Prep time: 15minutes
Cook time: 15minutes
Serving: 6
Temperature: Low

Ingredients:

- ➢ 1 watermelon, - cut into cubes
- ➢ 1 cantaloupe, - cut into cubes
- ➢ 1 pineapple, - cut into cubes
- ➢ 2 peaches, - cut into wedges
- ➢ balsamic vinegar, - to drizzle over the top
- ➢ 2 tbsp. fresh basil, - chopped
- ➢ salt, - to taste

Directions:

1. Light your grill and let it heat up.
2. Next, begin by chopping up every piece of fruit. The entire watermelon, cantaloupe, or pineapple won't be needed. Either chop it all up and preserve the leftovers or chop up roughly half of it. We used about a quarter of each watermelon, cantaloupe, and pineapple to make eight skewers.
3. Stuff your skewers full of chopped fruit. Although you could mix it up and put a little bit of everything on each skewer or do it the way we did, we chose to put the same fruit on each skewer for the photos.
4. Arrange the skewers on the grill when it is done. Grill each side for three to four minutes. The fruit should begin to blacken and soften, but not get very mushy. When done, take the food off the grill.
5. Place the fruit in a big serving dish after letting it cool, and your kabobs will become a salad. Add balsamic vinegar, then sprinkle fresh basil leaves on top of your salad. Enjoy!

NUTRITION: Calories: 104kCal: Fat: 17g: Protein: 1.27g: Carbs: 27g

91.   Grilled Plantains (Paleo + Whole30 Option)

Prep time: 5minutes
Cook time: 12minutes
Servings: 1/2
Temperature: medium

Ingredients:

- ➢ 4 very ripe plantains (should be almost black)
- ➢ 3 tbsp.s. coconut oil, melted
- ➢ Suggested toppings:
- ➢ Raw loCal honey, drizzled to taste, (omit for Whole30)
- ➢ Cinnamon, to taste
- ➢ Sea salt, to taste

Directions:

1. Preheat the grill to a temperature of about 500°.
2. Use a knife to score and peel plantain peels. Plantains should be split lengthwise.
3. Grill the plantains for 5-7 minutes on each side, basting often with melted coconut oil.
4. Take out, then top with your preferred seasonings and garnishes. Honey, cinnamon, and sea salt are our favorites. Enjoy!

NUTRITION: Calories: 168kCal: Fat: 4g: Protein: 1g: Carbs: 38g

92. Sesame Soy Grilled Tuna

Prep time: 2hrs
Cook time:
10minutes
Servings: 4
Temperature: Medium

Ingredients:

- 1/3 cup low-sodium soy sauce
- 3 tbsp. rice vinegar
- 2 green onions, chopped
- 1 garlic clove, minced
- 2 tsp sesame oil
- 1 tsp ginger, minced
- 1/2 tsp black pepper
- 24 oz.. ahi tuna steaks (about 6 oz.. each piece)
- 1 tbsp.. sesame seeds

Directions:

1. Combine the soy sauce, rice vinegar, green onions, garlic, sesame oil, ginger, and pepper. Soy sauce, green onions, garlic, ginger, and green onions are stirred in a bowl.
2. Marinate the tuna in this mixture in the refrigerator for at least 30 minutes, two hours or more is ideal. If you can, remove the tuna from the fridge twenty minutes before cooking so it can come to room temperature.
3. When ready to cook, remove the tuna from the marinade, brushing off any green onions. Brush the grill with oil or spray it with cooking spray. Cook the tuna for about 2 minutes on each side for medium rare. For medium well, cook about 4 minutes on each side.
4. Let rest for five minutes and slice with a sharp knife. Sprinkle with sesame seeds and serve.

NUTRITION: Calories: 237: Fat: 4g: Protein: 43g: Carbs: 4g

93.   Grilled Mahi Mahi

Prep time: 5minutes
Cook time: 10minutes
Servings: 6
Temperature: Medium

Ingredients:

- 24 oz. mahi mahi fillets (4 6-ounce fillets)
- 1 tbsp. olive oi
- 1 tsp paprika
- 1/2 tsp garlic powder
- 1/2 tsp onion powder
- 1/2 tsp cumin
- 1/2 tsp kosher salt
- 1/4 tsp black pepper

Directions:

1. Combine the paprika, garlic powder, onion powder, cumin, salt, and pepper.
2. Pat the mahi mahi fillets with paper towels to dry and remove any extra moisture. Brush the mahi mahi with olive oil. Coat with the spice rub
3. Make sure the grill is clean and oil if needed. Cook the fish for 4-5 minutes per side. Do not flip the fish too early, if it sticks it is likely not ready to flip. The fish is ready when it is opaque and flakes easily.

NUTRITION: Calories: 179: Fat: 5g: Protein: 32g: Carbs: 1g

94.   Easy Grilled Swordfish

Prep time: 15minutes
Cook time: 10minutes
Servings: 6
Temperature: Medium

Ingredients:

- ➤ 4 center-cut swordfish steaks (about 6 oz. each)
- ➤ 2 tbsp. olive oil
- ➤ 2 tbsp. low sodium soy sauce (or coconut aminos)
- ➤ 1 tbsp. lemon juice
- ➤ 1 garlic clove, minced
- ➤ 1 tsp Italian seasoning (or dried rosemary)
- ➤ 1/2 tsp black pepper

Directions:

1. Mix the olive oil, lemon juice, soy sauce, garlic, Italian seasoning, and black pepper.
2. Place the marinade in a shallow dish and add the fish. Turn to coat on both sides and let marinate for 15-20 minutes
3. Preheat the grill or a grill pan to medium-high heat. Remove the fish from the marinade. Use a fork to scrape off any garlic so it does not burn on the grill.
4. Cook the swordfish for 4-6 minutes on each side until the swordfish is cooked through and opaque. The exact cooking time will depend on the thickness and swordfish should be cooked to 145 degrees. Be careful not to overcook because swordfish can get dry quickly. Serve with fresh lemon.

NUTRITION: Calories: 247: Fat: 16g; Protein: 25g: Carbs: 1g

95.   Jalapeno Popper Chicken

Prep time: 5minutes
Cook time: 25minutes
Servings: 6
Temperature: Medium

Ingredients:

- ➤ 1.33 lbs. boneless skinless chicken breast, 4 pieces
- ➤ Salt and pepper
- ➤ 1/4 cup jalapenos, seeded and diced
- ➤ 2 oz. reduced-Fat cream cheese
- ➤ 3 tbsp. green onions, chopped
- ➤ 1/2 cup reduced-Fat shredded cheddar cheese

Directions:

1. Start by heating your oven or grill to 425 degrees.
2. Add salt and pepper to the chicken.
3. Grill it for about 7 to 10 minutes per side, or until fully done. The chicken should be baked in the oven for 25 to 30 minutes, or until the juices flow clear and the bird is thoroughly done.
4. In the meantime, combine the cheddar cheese, jalapenos, cream cheese, and green onions.
5. Take the cooked chicken and put it on a piece of foil for the grill. Return to the grill after spreading the cream cheese and jalapeño mixture on top. Grill the top tightly for 3-4 minutes, or until the cheese starts to melt.
6. To prepare the chicken for the oven, remove the baking dish and top it with the cream cheese-jalapeno mixture. Return to oven and cook 8-10 minutes or until cheese is creamy and melted.

NUTRITION: Calories: 226: Fat: 5g: Protein: 37g: Carbs: 2g

96.   Grilled Plum Salad with Goat Cheese

Prep time: 5minutes
Cook time: 10minutes
Servings: 4
Temperature: Medium

Directions:

- ➢ 4 plums (ripe but firm, pits removed and cut into 6 segments each)
- ➢ 1.5 tbsp. olive oil (dressing)
- ➢ 6 cups arugula
- ➢ 1/3 cup crumbled goat cheese
- ➢ 2 tbsp. mint, chopped
- ➢ 2 tbsp. basil, chopped
- ➢ 2 tbsp. red onion, thinly sliced
- ➢ 1 tbsp. lemon juice (dressing)
- ➢ 2 tsp honey (dressing)
- ➢ 2 tsp Dijon mustard (dressing)
- ➢ 1/16 tsp. red pepper flakes (dressing)
- ➢ Salt and pepper to taste

Directions:

1. Combine the dressing ingredients in a bowl and set aside.
2. Oil the grates of your grill or grill pan and preheat it to medium-high heat. For 1-2 minutes, or until grill marks form, cook the plums. For another two to three minutes, flip and grill. Set aside.
3. Combine the arugula, goat cheese, mint, basil, red onion, grilled plum pieces, and dressing to assemble the salad. When necessary, season with salt and pepper.

NUTRITION: Calories: 185: Fat: 13g: Protein: 6g: Carbs: 13g

97. Grilled Chicken with Mango Salsa

Prep time: 4 hours
Cook time:
15minutes
Servings: 6
Temperature: Low

Ingredients:

- 1.33 lbs. boneless skinless chicken breast
- 1/4 cup low sodium soy sauce (or coconut aminos)
- 2 tbsp. orange juice
- 1 tbsp. sesame oil
- 1 tbsp. honey (optional)
- 2 tsp. fresh ginger, minced
- 2 garlic cloves, minced
- 1/2 tsp. black pepper
- 1 mango, chopped
- 1/4 cup red onion, chopped
- 1/4 cup cilantro, chopped
- 1 lime juice only

Directions:

1. Slice the chicken breasts in half horizontally to create thinner cutlets. In a Ziploc bag, combine the chicken, and other ingredients. In the refrigerator, marinate for at least 4 hours.
2. Take the chicken out of the marinade and allow the excess to drip off before grilling. Put on a hot grill, and cook for three to five minutes on each side, or until done.
3. Combine the mango, red onion, cilantro, and lime juice to make the salsa. Add salt and pepper to taste. Overtop the grilled chicken, serve the salsa.

NUTRITION: Calories: 252: Fat: 6g: Protein: 34g: Carbs: 18g

98.   Grilled Plums

Prep time: 5minutes
Cook time: 10minutes
Servings: 1
Temperature: Medium

Ingredients:

- ➤ 4 plums (ripe but firm)
- ➤ 1 tbsp. butter, melted (I like salted or you can finish with sea salt)
- ➤ 1 tbsp. honey
- ➤ 1/2 tsp cinnamon
- ➤ 1/4 tsp vanilla extract

Directions:

1. After the butter has melted and become warm, stir in the honey, cinnamon, and vanilla essence. Set aside.
2. Oil the grates of your grill or grill pan and preheat it to medium-high heat. For 3 to 4 minutes, or until grill marks emerge, cook the fruit. For another two to three minutes, flip and grill.
3. Take the food off the grill and top it with honey butter. Serve with real whipped cream or froz.en yogurt (or whipped coconut cream).

NUTRITION: Calories: 73: Fat: 3g: Protein: 1g: Carbs: 12g

99.   Grilled Pineapple

Prep time: 15minutes
Cook time: 10minutes
Servings: 2
Temperature: Medium

Ingredients:

- ➢ 1 pineapple
- ➢ 3 tbsp. brown sugar
- ➢ 1 Salt to taste (flaky sea salt is best)

Directions:

1. Turn the grill's heat up to medium-high. To prevent sticking, make sure the grill is clean and oiled or sprayed with a grill spray.
2. Slice the pineapple into 1/2 to 3/4-inch-thick pieces after removing the rind and stem.
3. Sprinkle the slices with brown sugar and let them rest for at least 10 minutes.
4. Grill pineapple slices for 2-4 minutes per side, flipping once while cooking until they are tender, golden, and gently charred (the variation depends on the thickness, ripeness of pineapple, and actual heat of grill)

NUTRITION: Calories: 102Cal: Fat: 0g: Protein: 1g: Carbs: 27g

100. Grilled Avocados

Prep time: 5minutes
Cook time: 10minutes
Servings: 1/2
Temperature: Medium

Ingredients:

- ➤ 2 avocados, cut in half with pits removed
- ➤ 1/2 tbsp. olive oil
- ➤ Salt and pepper

Directions:

1. Season the avocado halves with salt and pepper after brushing them with oil.
2. Put on the grill, ensuring that the flesh side is facing up. Grill for 4-6 minutes or until grill marks turns brown. After three minutes, if desired, tilt the avocado slightly to create "X" grill markings.

NUTRITION: Calories: 176cal: Fat: 17g: Protein: 2g: Carbs: 9g

101. Pineapple Chicken Sausages

Prep time: 10minutes
Cook time: 10minutes
Servings: 1
Temperature: Medium

Ingredients:

- 4 chicken sausages (or vegetarian sausage
- 1 cup pineapple
- 1/2 cup red pepper, diced
- 1/2 jalapeno, diced
- 1/8 cup onion, diced
- 1/8 cup cilantro, diced
- 1/4 tsp. cumin
- 1/4 tsp. pepper
- 1 lime, juice

Directions:

1. Combine the lime, juice, cilantro, cumin, red pepper, jalapeño, onion, pineapple, and other ingredients in a bowl.
2. For precooked chicken sausages, grill the sausages for 6 to 8 minutes, per the instructions on the package.
3. Combine 1/4 cup light sour cream, 1/4 cup Greek yogurt, one seeded jalapeño, 1/4 cup cilantro, and a squeeze of lime juice to make a fast cilantro sauce. Add salt and pepper to taste.

NUTRITION: Calories: 175: Fat: 5g: Protein: 16g: Carbs: 12g

102. Blueberry Corn Salad with Honey-Lime Vinaigrette

Prep time: 10minutes
Cook time: 10minutes
Servings: ¾ cup
Temperature: Low

Ingredients:

- ➢ 3 ears of fresh corn
- ➢ 1 cup blueberries
- ➢ 1/4 cup red onion, diced
- ➢ 1/4 cup cilantro, chopped
- ➢ 1/2 jalapeno pepper, seeded and diced
- ➢ 1 tbsp. lime juice
- ➢ 1 tbsp. olive oil
- ➢ 1/2 tbsp. honey
- ➢ 1/4 tsp salt
- ➢ 1/4 tsp black pepper
- ➢ 1/8 tsp cumin

Directions:

1. Grill the corn for 8 to 10 minutes, turning it over a few times, or until it is gently browned all over. Separate the corn from its husk.
2. To make the dressing, combine the lime, juice, cumin, honey, olive oil, salt, and pepper.
3. Combine the dressing with all the ingredients. If necessary, season with salt and pepper.

NUTRITION: Calories: 125Cal: Carbs: 22g: Fat: 4g: Protein: 3g

103. Cajun Salmon

Prep time: 5minutes
Cook time: 10minutes
Servings: 4
Temperature: Medium

Ingredients:

- 4 tbsp. paprika
- 1 tbsp. garlic powder
- 1 tbsp. onion powder
- 1 tbsp. salt
- 1 tbsp. pepper
- 1.5 tsp dried thyme
- 1/2 tsp cayenne (adjust to preference)

Directions:

1. To make the Cajun seasoning, combine the spices. Olive oil should be brushed on the salmon before seasoning the flesh side.
2. Heat the broiler while keeping the oven rack about 6 inches from the heat. To make cleanup easier, place the salmon on a baking sheet lined with foil. For it to be barely cooked through and flaky, broil for 6 to 8 minutes.
3. Grill: Put the salmon on a hot grill skin side down. Sauté for 3 to 4 minutes or until nearly done. Cook until done, flipping after one to three minutes.
4. Pan Seared: Heat a heavy bottomed pan or cast iron skillet over medium-high heat.

NUTRITION: Calories: 350: Carbs: 1g: Fat: 24g: Protein:

104. Baked Haddock with Seafood Stuffing

Prep time: 10minutes
Cook time: 10minutes
Servings: 6
Temperature: Medium

Ingredients:

- 1.33 lbs. haddock (or other fish)
- 3/4 cup Panko breadcrumbs (or crushed crackers)
- 1/2 cup imitation crab meat, diced
- 2 tbsp. butter, melted
- 2 tbsp. lemon juice
- 1 tbsp. parsley
- 1/2 tsp. salt
- 1/2 tsp. pepper

Directions:

1. Increase oven temperature to 500 degrees. Although you might broil the fish, an oven rack allows the fish to cook more uniformly. The fish can also be grilled on a piece of foil.
2. Combine the butter, parsley, lemon juice, crab, and breadcrumbs.
3. Apply the fish with filling. Cook the fish for 5-7 minutes on a baking pan in the oven, or until it flakes easily. On the grill, it ought to take about the same amount of time.
4. To grill, lay a sizable sheet of sturdy aluminum foil over the fish before placing it on the grill. Grill the salmon for 5-7 minutes, or until it is flaky and thoroughly cooked.

NUTRITION: Calories: 245: Fat: 7g: Carbs: 9g: Protein: 26g

105. Hoisin Asian Salmon

Prep time: 5minutes
Cook time: 10minutes
Servings: 4
Temperature: Medium

Ingredients:

- 1 lb. salmon (wild is best)
- 3 tbsp. Hoisin sauce
- 2 tsp. low sodium soy sauce
- 1 garlic clove, minced
- 1 tsp. minced ginger
- 1/2 tsp Sriracha

Directions:

1. Set the broiler on high.
2. Combine the Hoisin, soy sauce, ginger, garlic, and garlic. Add 1-4 teaspoons of Sriracha if you want your food hot. You can also apply this individually to the servings of fish you would want to be hotter.
3. Apply the Hoisin sauce mixture to the fish. Put on a baking pan with foil on it.
4. Position the fish 6 inches or so from the broiler. Depending on the thickness of the fish, broil for 5 to 10 minutes or until opaque and flaky. Instead, you can cook for 8-12 minutes at 500 degrees.

NUTRITION: Calories: 265: Fat: 16g: Carbs: 6g: Protein: 24g

106. Mexican Street Corn

Prep time: 5minutes
Cook time: 10minutes
Servings: 4
Temperature: Medium

Directions:

- ➢ 4 ears of corn
- ➢ ¼ cup of crema Mexican agria sour cream
- ➢ ¼ cup of mayonnaise
- ➢ ½ cup of cotija cheese, crumbled
- ➢ 2 cloves of garlic, crushed
- ➢ ½ teaspoon of fine sea salt.
- ➢ Juice and zest of one lime.
- ➢ ¼ cup of cilantro finely chopped.

Directions:

1. Just tenderize the corn on the cob. For this meal, grilling corn is the ideal method of Prep. Take off the husks and silk before grilling the corn. Put there, then cover the grill. Flip approximately every 5 minutes until cooked and starting to brown in spots.
2. Combine the salt, pepper, garlic powder, sour cream, mayonnaise, and it in a bowl. On each ear of corn, apply a thin layer of the mayo mixture.
3. Add some chili spice and queso fresco on top. Add some freshly squeezed lime juice.

NUTRITION: Calories: 201: Fat: 9g: Carbs:30g:Protein:7g

107. Carne Asada

Prep time: 2 hours
Cook time: 20minutes
Servings: 4
Temperature: Medium

Ingredients:

- 1.33 lbs. lean flank steak
- 2 limes, juice
- 1 orange, juiced
- 4 garlic cloves, minced
- 1 jalapeno, minced
- 1 cup cilantro, chopped
- 2 tbsp. white vinegar
- 2 tbsp.. olive oil
- Salt and pepper

Directions:

1. Combine the olive oil, vinegar, garlic, cilantro, lime juice, orange juice, salt, and pepper.
2. Marinate the steak in this mixture for no more than 8 hours in the refrigerator, but no less than 2 hours. Over 8 hours of marinating will result in mushy meat.
3. When you are ready to grill, heat up the grill to medium. If preferred, cook the steak for 6 to 8 minutes on each side. Slice thin after allowing resting for five minutes.
4. Let the carne aside rest for five minutes. Slice against the grain very thinly. Serve with lime juice and fresh cilantro.

NUTRITION: Calories: 324: Fat: 16g: Carbs: 11g: Protein: 34g

108. Spanish Flank Steak

Prep time: 1 hour
Cook time: 10minutes
Servings: 4
Temperature: Medium

Ingredients:

- 1 lb. lean flank steak
- 2 tbsp. olive oil
- 2 tbsp. sherry vinegar
- 2 tbsp. low sodium soy sauce
- 2 garlic cloves, minced
- 1 tsp. dried rosemary
- 1 tsp. dried oregano
- Salt and pepper
- 1 cup cherry tomatoes, chopped
- 1/4 cup red onion, diced
- 2 tbsp. fresh basil, chopped (or parsley, oregano)

Directions:

1. To help it become softer, prick the steak all over with a fork. Garlic, rosemary, oregano, half the olive oil, half the balsamic vinegar, and salt and pepper to taste should be sprinkled over top. Marinate overnight or for at least one hour.

2. Toss the red onion, tomatoes, and basil together before serving. If you like, add a little sherry vinegar and olive oil. Add salt and pepper to taste.

3. Broil or grill the steaks as desired: For medium rare, cook for 4-6 minutes on each side.

1. A broiler pan should be covered in foil to broil. With the extra marinade dripping off, remove the steak from the solution. For medium, place the steak in the center of the rack and cook for 4-6 minutes on each side.

4. Let rest for 5 minutes and then thinly slice against the grain. Add tomato salad or chimichurri on top.

NUTRITION: Calories: 254: Fat: 14g: Carbs: 5g: Protein: 26g

109. Cumin Chicken

Prep time: 5minutes
Cook time: 10minutes
Servings: 6
Temperature: Medium

Ingredients:

- 1.5 lbs. boneless skinless chicken breast
- 1 tbsp.. olive oil
- 1 tsp. cumin
- 1 tsp garlic powder
- 1/2 tsp. paprika
- 1/2 tsp. kosher salt
- 1/4 tsp. black pepper
- 1/4 tsp. red pepper flakes (optional)
- 1 lime (or lemon, for serving)

Directions:

1. Turn the heat to medium-high and prepare the grill or grill pan. In a small bowl, combine the cumin, garlic powder, paprika, salt, pepper, and red pepper flakes.
2. Olive oil should be brushed on the chicken breasts. To uniformly coat the chicken, sprinkle it over and give it a good massage.
3. Grill each side for 4-6 minutes, or until thoroughly done. Wrap in foil and allow to rest for five minutes. Add freshly squeezed lime juice to the dish

NUTRITION: Calories: 189: Fat: 4g: Carbs: 0g:Protein:32g

110. Grilled Cilantro Lime Chicken

Prep time: 1 hour
Cook time: 15min
Servings: 6
Temperature: Medium

Ingredients:

- 1.33 lbs. boneless skinless chicken breasts
- 1/2 cup cilantro
- 1/3 cup lime juice
- 2 tbsp. olive oil
- 2 tbsp. water
- 2 garlic cloves, minced
- 1 tbsp. brown sugar (leave out for low carb/Paleo/Whole30)
- 1 tsp. salt
- 1 tsp. pepper
- 1/2 tsp. cumin
- 1/2 tsp. red pepper flakes

Directions:

1. Make thick cutlets or strips out of the chicken. To a food processor or blender, add the cilantro, lime juice, olive oil, water, brown sugar, salt, pepper, cumin, and red pepper flakes. Pulse until combined. Chicken should be marinated in the remaining sauce for at least an hour after setting aside half of it.
2. Marinate the chicken in the remaining sauce for at least an hour, setting aside half of it.
3. Take the chicken out of the marinade and allow the excess to drip off before grilling. Grill the chicken for 4-6 minutes on each side, or until cooked through. Serve the chicken with any residual sauce.

NUTRITION: Calories: 250: Fat: 9g: Carbs: 6g: Protein: 32g

111. Blackstone Garlic Butter Lamb

Prep time:
5minutes Cook
time: 15minutes
Servings: 1
Temperature: High

Ingredients:

- 1 package of French Lamb Ribs or Lamb Chops
- 1 teaspoon salt
- 1/2 teaspoon black pepper
- 1 teaspoon minced garlic
- 8 tablespoons room temperature butter
- 1/4 cup fresh herbs, including parsley, mint, and oregano

Directions:

1. Combine the room-temperature butter, salt, pepper, and diced herbs in a small bowl. After that, cover the lamb with it.
2. Turn the griddle's heat to medium-high or high. After that, put the lamb on the griddle, where it will immediately sear. The amount of time required for cooking depends on the thickness of the chops and your preference for the cooking temperature. I spent 3-5 minutes on each side.
3. Let your lamb chops 5 to 10 minutes to rest before eating.
4. Dish up, serve, and savor!

NUTRITION: Calories: 290: Fat: 21g: Carbs: 1g: Protein: 7g

112. Keto Grilled Radishes

Prep time: 5
Cook time: 15
Servings: 1
Temperature: Medium

Ingredients:

- ➤ 16 oz. Radishes
- ➤ 2 tbsp. olive oil
- ➤ 1 tsp fresh rosemary or any of your favorite seasoning combinations listed above
- ➤ 1 tsp pink salt

Directions:

1. Wash the radishes first.
2. Dice or quarter the radishes.
3. Warm up the Blackstone griddle grill over medium heat.
4. Add the olive oil after it has warmed up.
5. Put the hot griddle with the washed radishes on it.
6. Grill the radishes for 5 to 7 minutes on each side or until fork-tender, then sprinkle with fresh rosemary.
7. Sprinkle pink salt on top, then serve hot.

NUTRITION: Calories: 76: Fat: 7.1g: Carbs: 3g: Protein: 1.2g

113. Blackstone Griddle Sausage & Mushroom Flatbread Pizza

Prep time: 10minutes
Cook time: 15minutes
Servings: 1
Temperature: Medium

Ingredients:

- 2 Flatbread Crusts
- 6 ounces of ground Italian sausage, hot or mild
- 1/2 cup prepared pesto
- 2 cups diced mushrooms, any type
- 1/2 cup sautéed onions (regular)
- 1 cup shredded Mozzarella cheese

Directions:

1. Place the flatbread crust down, add some pesto to the bottom, and then top with your cooked sliced onions, ground sausage, and diced mushrooms.
2. Place the flatbread on top of the Blackstone Griddle after preheating the grill to medium-high. Cook for 10 to 15 minutes until it is thoroughly done.
3. Plate, present, and indulge!

NUTRITION: Calories: 1082: Fat: 70g: Carbs: 72g: Protein: 45g

114. Marinated Caprese Chicken

Prep time: 20minutes
Cook time: 22minutes
Servings: 6
Temperature: Medium

Ingredients:

- ➤ Six boneless, skinless, chicken breasts.
- ➤ 1 cup Italian dressing
- ➤ 8 ounces fresh mozzarella, sliced
- ➤ 2 tomatoes, sliced
- ➤ ½ cup basil, chopped
- ➤ 1/3 cup balsamic glaze

Directions:

1. Add Italian dressing to a sealable plastic bag with chicken breasts. Stir to ensure a uniform coating, then marinate for 1 to 12 hours in the refrigerator.
2. Add a thin layer of olive oil to the griddle and heat it to medium-high.
3. Take the chicken out of the marinade and griddle it for about 5 minutes on each side (internal temperature should reach 165 degrees).
4. Add freshly sliced mozzarella cheese to the chicken during the final 3 minutes of cooking, then finish off the process.
5. After removing the chicken from the griddle, top it with tomato slices and add balsamic glaze and basil sprigs as desired.

NUTRITION: Calories: 562: Fat: 28g: Carbs: 13g: Protein: 62g

115. Grilled Peaches with Vanilla Ice Cream

Prep time: 20minutes
Cook time: 20minutes
Servings: 4
Temperature: Medium

Directions:

- ¾ cup balsamic vinegar
- 3 tablespoons white sugar
- 2 teaspoons freshly ground black peppercorns
- 2 large fresh peaches with peel, halved, and pitted
- 2 ½ ounces blue cheese, crumbled

Directions:

1. Start by preparing your glaze: Combine the ingredients for the glaze in a small bowl and set aside.
2. Combine the olive oil, honey, and cinnamon in a small bowl.
3. Brush Open Halves of Peaches with Cinnamon Honey Mixture
4. Grill should be heated to between 350 and 400 degrees.
5. Place peaches on the grill, open side down, and cook for 3-4 minutes.
6. Grill the peaches for a further 3-4 minutes after turning them 90 degrees.
7. Serve right away with cinnamon glaze and fresh vanilla ice cream!

NUTRITION: Calories: 147: Fat: 5g: Carbs: 21g: Protein: 4g

116. Grilled Asian Cod

Prep time: 10minutes
Cook time: 10minutes
Servings: 2
Temperature: Medium

Ingredients:

- 12 ounces thick-cut cod
- ½ cup orange juice
- ⅓ cup reduced-sodium soy sauce
- 2 tablespoons lemon juice
- 2 tablespoons brown sugar
- 2 tablespoons chopped green onions
- 2 teaspoons ginger paste
- 2 teaspoons minced garlic

Directions:

1. Fill a freezer bag with a gallon's worth of cod. Brown sugar, green onions, ginger paste, orange juice, soy sauce, lemon juice, and garlic are added: everything is combined after that. Seal the bag after removing the extra air. For at least two hours, marinate food in the refrigerator.
2. Lightly oil the grate of an outdoor grill and heat it to medium-high. Cod should be cooked in a grill basket on a hot grill for 7 to 9 minutes, or until it achieves an internal temperature of 135 degrees F (57 degrees C).

NUTRITION: Calories: 268: Fat: 2g: Carbs: 30g: Protein: 34g

117. Grilled Tuna Steaks with Grape and Caper Salsa

Prep time: 20minutes
Cook time: 5minutes
Servings: 4
Temperature: Medium

Ingredients:

- cups red seedless grape, halved
- ⅓ cup capers, drained and rinsed
- 1 shallot, minced
- 2 tablespoons chopped fresh parsley
- 1 tablespoon olive oil
- salt and black pepper to taste
- 4 (8-ounce) tuna steaks
- ¼ cup fresh lemon juice

Directions:

1. Heat a grill outside to medium-high and give the grates a light oiling.
2. Combine the grapes, capers, shallot, parsley, and olive oil in a bowl. Add salt and pepper to taste, and set the bowl aside. On a platter, arrange the tuna steaks and drizzle them with lemon juice. To taste, add salt and pepper to the food.
3. On a prepared grill, cook tuna steaks for two to three minutes per side for medium-rare, or until they reach the desired degree of doneness. Salsa of grapes and capers is recommended.

NUTRITION: Calories: 348: Fat: 6g: Carbs: 18g: Protein: 54g

118. Grilled Halibut with Cilantro Garlic Butter

Prep time: 25minutes
Cook time: 8minutes
Servings: 4
Temperature: Medium

Ingredients:

- 4 (6-ounce) fillets of halibut
- 1 lime, cut into wedges
- salt and pepper to taste
- 3 cloves garlic, coarsely chopped
- ½ cup chopped fresh cilantro
- 1 tablespoon fresh lime juice
- 2 tablespoons butter
- 1 tablespoon olive oil

Directions:

1. Turn the grill's heat to high. Add salt and pepper to the fish fillets after squeezing the lime wedges' juice over them.

2. Cook fish fillets for approximately five minutes per side, or until they are browned and easily flaked with a fork to a warm serving platter after removal.

3. In a skillet set over medium heat, warm the oil. Add the garlic and whisk briefly for 2 minutes, or until it begins to smell good. Add the remaining lime juice, cilantro, and butter. With the cilantro butter sauce, serve the fish.

NUTRITION: Calories: 276: Fat: 13g: Carbs: 3g: Protein: 35g

119. Grilled Tuna with Fresh Horseradish

Prep time: 5minutes
Cook time: 6minutes
Servings: 2
Temperature: High

Ingredients:

- 2 (8-ounce) fresh tuna steaks
- 1 teaspoon vegetable oil
- 2 tablespoons soy sauce
- 2 tablespoons seasoned rice vinegar
- 1 tablespoon finely grated raw horseradish root, or more to taste
- 4 cherry tomatoes, sliced
- ½ teaspoon hot Chile paste (such as sambal oilec)
- 1 tablespoon minced green onion

Directions:

1. Lightly oil the grate of an outside grill and preheat it to high heat. Use vegetable oil to sparingly coat steaks.
2. In a bowl, combine the soy sauce, rice vinegar, horseradish, cherry tomatoes, and hot Chile paste. Give it 20 minutes to sit.
3. Grill steaks for 3 minutes per side over the hotter area of the grill. Place on a platter. Steaks should be covered with the soya sauce mixture and topped with green onions.

NUTRITION: Calories: 288: Fat: 5g: Carbs: 4g: Protein: 54g

120. Grilled Trout

Prep time: 15minutes
Cook time: 15minutes
Servings: 4
Temperature: High

Ingredients:

- ➤ 2 whole trout, cleaned
- ➤ 1 tablespoon olive oil, divided
- ➤ 1 pinch of coarse sea salt to taste
- ➤ 1 pinch of ground black pepper
- ➤ ½ lemon, thinly sliced
- ➤ ½ sweet onion, thinly sliced
- ➤ 1 clove garlic, minced
- ➤ 2 sprigs of fresh rosemary
- ➤ 2 sprigs of fresh thyme

Directions:

1. Lightly oil the grate of an outside grill and preheat it to high heat.
2. Liberally apply olive oil and sea salt to the outside of each trout.
3. Add salt and black pepper to the cavities. Add minced garlic, a sprig of rosemary and thyme, and half each of the lemon and onion slices to the cavity of each trout.
4. Lower the heat to low and set the trout directly on the grill. Cook for 6 to 7 minutes per side, flipping once, or until the flesh flakes easily.

NUTRITION: Calories: 242: Fat: 11g: Carbs: 4g: Protein: 31g

121. Cajun Blackened Catfish

Prep time: 10minutes
Cook time: 10minutes
Servings: 4
Temperature: High

Directions:

- ➢ 1 teaspoon kosher salt
- ➢ 1 teaspoon ground black pepper
- ➢ 1 teaspoon ground cayenne pepper
- ➢ 1 teaspoon garlic powder
- ➢ 1 teaspoon onion powder
- ➢ 1 teaspoon paprika
- ➢ 1 teaspoon dried parsley
- ➢ ½ teaspoon dried oregano
- ➢ ½ teaspoon dried thyme
- ➢ 4 (4 ounces) catfish fillets, skinned
- ➢ ¾ cup unsalted butter

Directions:

1. In a small bowl, add salt, black and cayenne pepper, garlic powder, onion powder, paprika, parsley, oregano, and thyme. Catfish fillets should be pressed into the spice mixture to coat completely.
2. In a basin, liquefy the butter and save.
3. Set up a portable heat source outside, such as a butane burner or a gas grill's side burner. After lighting the burner, set a sizable cast-iron pan on it and turn the heat to high. Add roughly 1/4 cup of melted butter into the skillet.
4. Add catfish fillets to the skillet after the butter in it is sizzling hot. Fry for about 3 minutes on each side, or until the spices are burnt onto the fillets and the catfish is opaque and flaky within. Avoid breathing in the smoke.
5. To serve, cover the catfish with the remaining 1/2 cup of butter.

NUTRITION: Calories: 466: Fat: 43g: Carbs: 2g: Protein: 18g

122. Caprese Mac & Cheese

Prep time: 20minutes
Cook time: 15minutes
Servings: 4
Temperature: Medium

Ingredients:

- 1 (24-ounce) package of elbow macaroni, cooked
- 1 (10-ounce) package of grape tomatoes
- 1 red bell pepper, diced
- 1 (13.5-ounce) can of spinach (squeeze out any excess liquid)
- 1 (6.5-ounce) jar basil pesto sauce
- Salt and pepper, to taste
- 1 cup heavy cream
- 1 (16-ounce) package of shredded mozzarella
- Vegetable oil, for the griddle

Directions:

1. Bring the Blackstone griddle's heat to medium. After adding the diced pepper, tomatoes, and spinach, drizzle some vegetable oil. Add salt and pepper to taste. The tomatoes should be faintly blistered after 3-4 minutes of cooking the vegetables on the griddle top.
2. Include the cooked pasta in the pan. With the aid of a spatula, combine the pasta and vegetables thoroughly.
3. Cover the pasta with pesto, heavy cream, and cheese. To create a thick, cheesy sauce, stir with spatulas. Serve right away after taking the food off the griddle.

NUTRITION: Calories: 591: Fat: 32g: Carbs: 52g: Protein: 18g

123. Game Day Nachos

Prep time: 20minutes
Cook time: 30minutes
Servings: 4
Temperature: Medium

Directions:

- ➢ 1 large tomato, diced
- ➢ 1/2 red onion, diced
- ➢ 2 limes, juiced
- ➢ Of 1 bunch of cilantro, chopped
- ➢ Of 1 packet of fajita seasoning
- ➢ 1 pound 80/20 ground beef
- ➢ 1 (15-ounce) can of black beans, drained
- ➢ 1 large bag of corn tortilla chips
- ➢ 1 (16-ounce) package of shredded fiesta blend cheese
- ➢ 1 (12-ounce) can of pickled jalapeños
- ➢ 1 cup sour cream, transferred into a squirt bottle
- ➢ 2 avocados, sliced
- ➢ Salt and pepper, to taste
- ➢ Vegetable oil, for the griddle

Directions:

1. Create the Pico de Gallo first. In a medium mixing bowl, combine the tomato, red onion, lime juice, and cilantro. Add salt and pepper to taste after stirring. Set aside.
2. Turn the Blackstone griddle's heat to medium. Oil the pan with vegetables, and then add the ground meat. Cook until browned after adding the fajita-seasoning packet. Add the black beans and a sizable portion of the previously prepared Pico de Gallo. Stir continuously until the beans are thoroughly heated.
3. Reduce the griddle's heat to low. On the griddle, arrange the tortilla chips, shredded cheese, pickled jalapenos, and ground beef mixture with black beans. For ten minutes, keep covered with a sizable basting dome or the griddle hood.
4. Place the nachos on a sizable serving dish after removing them from the griddle. It is time to get serious about your business. Serve right away.

NUTRITION: Calories: 702: Fat: 44g: Carbs: 26g: Protein: 49g

124. Coconut Shrimp

Prep time: 15minutes
Cook time: 10minutes
Servings: 6
Temperature: Medium

Ingredients:

For the Shrimp:

- ➤ 1 pound large, extra-large, or jumbo shrimp
- ➤ 1 cup all-purpose flour, divided
- ➤ 1/2 tablespoon Blackstone Citrus Garlic Mojo Seasoning
- ➤ 1 bottle of beer
- ➤ 2 cups unsweetened coconut flakes
- ➤ Oil for frying

For the Dipping Sauce:

- ➤ 1/2 cup orange marmalade
- ➤ 1 tablespoon horseradish
- ➤ 1 tablespoon stone ground mustard

Directions:

1. Combine the ingredients for the dipping sauce in a small bowl, adjusting the quantities to your taste (e.g. adding more horseradish for a stronger flavor or more marmalade for a sweeter sauce). Keep chilled until you are ready to serve.
2. Butterfly the shrimp after peeling them but keeping the tails on.
3. Combine 1 cup of flour and the Blackstone Citrus Garlic Mojo seasoning in a gallon-sized storage bag. To uniformly coat the shrimp, add them to the bag and shake it lightly.
4. Create a batter-like consistency with 1 cup of flour and enough beer in a sizable mixing basin. Set aside.
5. Add the coconut flakes to a second sizable mixing bowl.
6. Put each shrimp into the beer batter one at a time, letting the excess drip off. After that, push the shrimp into the coconut flakes to coat them completely. Repeat the process until all of the shrimp are coated, then place the coated shrimp on a tray lined with parchment paper. Before frying, freeze the shrimp tray for at least 20 to 30 minutes.
7. Get the oil's temperature up to 350 degrees. The shrimp should be fried in batches for two to three minutes on each side, or until golden brown. The shrimp should be allowed to dry on paper towels.
8. Spoon the dipping sauce and additional seasoning over the shrimp before serving. Enjoy!

NUTRITION: Calories: 1166: Fat: 118g: Carbs: 26g: Protein: 4g

125. Monte Cristo

Prep time: 10minutes
Cook time: 5minutes
Servings: 4
Temperature: Medium

Ingredients:

- 12 thick-cut slices sourdough bread or Texas toast
- 6 eggs, beaten
- 1 cup half and half
- 18 ounces of thinly sliced smoked ham
- 12 slices Swiss cheese
- Vegetable oil, for the griddle
- Strawberry jam, to serve

Directions:

1. Make the batter first. The half-&-half and beaten eggs are whisked together. In a casserole dish or a big basin, pour the mixture.
2. Turn the Blackstone griddle's heat to medium. Six equal chunks of ham should be placed on the griddle top along with some vegetable oil. The ham should be roasted all the way through after 2 minutes on each side, and the edges should begin to crisp up.
3. Coat both sides of the bread slices with the egg batter by dipping them into it. While the ham is cooking, place it on the griddle and cook for 2 minutes on each side. Spread strawberry jam on each slice of bread after the first side has finished cooking.
4. Add two slices of Swiss cheese on top of each ham serving. For one minute, or until the cheese is completely melted, cover with a basting dome. Use your spatulas to spread the meat onto the bread after the cheese has melted, and then add another slice on top. You will receive a total of 6 sandwiches.
5. After taking the sandwiches off the griddle, slice them in half, and serve right away.

NUTRITION: Calories: 641: Fat: 34g: Carbs: 33g: Protein: 49g

126. Colorado Cajun

Prep time:
10minutes
Cook time:
25minutes
Servings: 4
Temperature: High

Ingredients:

- Extra virgin olive oil or other cooking oil, for the griddle
- 3 tablespoons garlic paste
- 4 fully cooked Cajun style Andouille sausage, sliced (recommend Aid ells brand), chopped
- 1 cup yellow onion, chopped
- 1 cup red bell pepper, chopped
- 1 cup celery, chopped
- 3 bags of Ben's pre-cooked Long Grain Wild Ready Rice
- Blackstone Bayou Blend Seasoning, to taste
- 1-2 cups heavy whipping cream
- Cajun hot sauce (optional)
- 1 bunch parsley, chopped
- 1 lemon, halved

Directions:

1. Start by turning the Blackstone Griddle's heat up high.
2. Oil the griddle surface by drizzling and spreading it. Lay down the sausage and the garlic paste. Until the sausage is caramelized, combine and cook.
3. Add celery, onion, and bell peppers. Together with the sausage, sauté the vegetables until they are tender but still have some crunch (a little crunch is excellent!).
4. Combine the ingredients for the rice.
5. Blackstone's Bayou Blend is used to season everything. Cream cheese and Cajun hot sauce should be added (optional).
6. Add lemon juice and parsley before removing from the griddle.
7. Enjoy!

NUTRITION: Calories: 516: Fat: 29g: Carbs: 32g: Protein: 29g

127. Honey Dijon Grilled Artichokes

Prep time: 15 minutes
Cooking time: 15 minutes
Servings: 4
Temperature: MEDIUM & LOW

Ingredients:

- 6 whole artichokes, cut into half lengthwise
- 1/2-gallon water
- 3 tbsp. sea salt
- olive oil, as needed
- sea salt to taste
- 1/4 cup raw honey
- 1/4 cup boiling water
- 3 tbsp. Dijon mustard

Directions:

1. Mix the 3 tablespoons of sea salt and water. Place the artichokes in the brine for 30 minutes to several hours before cooking. Heat the griddle grill to medium heat.
2. Remove the artichokes from the brine, drizzle with olive oil on the cut side, and season with sea salt. Grill for 15 minutes on each side: cut side down first.
3. Turn the grill down to low, and turn the artichokes cut-side down while you mix the honey, boiling water, and Dijon.
4. Turn the artichokes back over, and brush the Dijon mix well over the cut side until it is all absorbed.

NUTRITION: Calories: 601, Fat: 57 g, Protein: 8 g, Carbs: 21 g

128. Carrots with Maple-Glazed

Prep time: 5 minutes
Cooking time: 6 minutes
Servings: 4
Temperature: Medium

Ingredients:

- ➤ 2 lb. carrots, peeled and trimmed
- ➤ 1 tbsp. olive oil
- ➤ Salt and pepper to taste
- ➤ 1 tbsp. maple syrup

Directions:

1. Preheat the griddle to medium heat and heat the oil.
2. Brush the carrot with olive oil and season with salt and pepper to taste. Place on the griddle pan and cook for 3 minutes on each side.
3. Brush with maple syrup before serving.

NUTRITION: Calories: 89: Protein: 2 g: Carbs: 14 g: Fat: 4 g

129. Sugar Snap Peas

Prep time: 15 minutes
Cook time: 10 minutes
Servings: 4
Temperature: High

Ingredients:

- 2-pound sugar snap peas end trimmed
- ½ tsp garlic powder
- 1 tsp salt
- 2/3 tsp ground black pepper
- 2 tbsp. olive oil

Directions:

1. Preheat the griddle to high heat.
2. Meanwhile, take a medium bowl, place peas in it add garlic powder and oil, season with salt and black pepper, toss until mixed, and then spread on the sheet pan.
3. When the griddle has preheated, open the lid, place the prepared sheet pan on the griddle grate, shut the griddle, and smoke for 10 minutes until slightly charred. Serve straight away.

NUTRITION: Calories: 60, Carbs: 7g, Fat: 0g, Protein: 2g

130. Zucchini Noodles

Prep time: 10 minutes
Cooking time: 12 minutes
Servings: 4
Temperature: High

Ingredients:

- ➢ 4 small zucchinis, spiralized
- ➢ 1 tbsp. soy sauce
- ➢ 2 onions, spiralized
- ➢ 2 tbsp. olive oil
- ➢ 1 tbsp. sesame seeds
- ➢ 2 tbsp. teriyaki sauce

Directions:

1. Preheat the griddle to high heat, and add oil to the hot griddle top.

2. Add onion and sauté for 4-5 minutes. Add zucchini noodles and cook for 2 minutes.

3. Add sesame seeds, teriyaki sauce, and soy sauce, and cook for 4-5 minutes. Serve and enjoy.

NUTRITION: Calories: 124: Fat: 8.4g: Carbs: 11.3 g: Protein: 3.2 g

131. Griddle Spicy Tofu

Prep time: 10minutes
Cook time: 8minutes
Servings: 4
Temperature: High

Ingredients:

- 1 lb. firm tofu, pressed & cut into 3/4-inch-thick slices
- 1 tsp soy sauce
- 1 tbsp. hoisin sauce
- 2 tbsp. olive oil
- ¼ tsp garlic powder
- 1 tsp chili powder
- ¼ tsp ground pepper
- 1 tsp ground cumin
- ¼ tsp salt
- Cooking spray

Directions:

1. Add the tofu slices and the remaining
2. Ingredients into the mixing bowl and mix well and let it sit for 10 minutes– Pre-heat the griddle to high heat.
3. Spray the griddle top with cooking spray. Place the tofu slices on a hot griddle top and cook for 3-4 minutes on each side. Serve and enjoy.

NUTRITION: Calories: 154, Fat: 12.1 g, Carbs: 4.6 g, Protein: 9.7 g

132. Butter Pepper Asparagus Spears

Prep time: 15 minutes
Cooking time: 10 minutes
Servings: 4
Temperature:

Ingredients:

- 1½ pounds thick asparagus spears, trimmed
- 3 tbsp. butter, melted
- Salt & black pepper to taste

Directions:

1. Preheat the griddle to medium heat. Grease the griddle top with cooking spray.
2. Drizzle melted butter over asparagus and season with salt and black pepper as needed.
3. Arrange asparagus on the hot griddle top and cook for 10 minutes. Serve warm.

NUTRITION: Calories 117, Fat 5.8 g, Carbs 9.9g, Protein 6.7g

133. Griddle Collard Green with Bacon

Prep time: 15 minutes
Cooking time: 30 minutes
Servings: 4
Temperature: Medium

Ingredients:

- 1-pound shredded collard greens
- 8 strips of thick-cut bacon
- 1/3 cup chopped yellow onion
- ½ cup chicken stock
- 2 tbsp. red wine vinegar
- 2 tsp red pepper flake
- Black pepper and salt, to taste
- Olive oil, as needed

Directions:

1. Grease the griddle with cooking spray and preheat to medium heat.
2. Add the bacon to the griddle top, and cook for 5-6 minutes, or until well cooked and crisp.
3. Drain on a few pieces of paper towel after removing from the griddle.
4. Cook the onion for 4-5 minutes on the skillet, stirring frequently. Toss in the collard greens with a touch of salt and a huge pinch of pepper to combine.
5. Cook, frequently tossing, for 4-5 minutes. Cover with a dome and 12 cups of chicken stock. Cook for a total of 3-4 minutes.
6. Combine the remaining chicken stock, red wine vinegar, and red pepper flake in a large mixing bowl.
7. Toss to ensure that all of the fixings are uniformly distributed. Cover and then let it cook for4-5 minutes before serving. Serve.

NUTRITION: Calories 317: Fat 32g: Carbs 12g: Protein 22g

134. Griddle Candied Sausage Sweet Potatoes

Prep time: 15 minutes
Cooking time: 10 minutes
Servings: 4
Temperature: Medium-Low

Ingredients:

- ➢ 4 large sweet potatoes, diced small
- ➢ 1 lb. savory sage ground sausage
- ➢ 2 tbsp. oil
- ➢ 5 tbsp. butter, unsalted
- ➢ 1 cup brown sugar
- ➢ Black pepper and salt, to taste
- ➢ Dried parsley, as needed

Directions:

1. Place sweet potatoes in your large mixing bowl and dice them into small pieces. Season with black pepper and salt and toss to coat with oil lightly.
2. Preheat the griddle to medium-low heat. Simmer the sausage and crumble on one side while the potatoes cook on the other.
3. In the center of the sausage and potato mixture, make a well. Melt the butter in the center, then stir in the brown sugar.
4. Add a little sprinkle of parsley, and then let it cook for another one-two minutes. Serve.

NUTRITION: Calories 304: Fat 14.9g: Carbs 12g: Protein 21g

135. Griddle Cheesy Leeks

Prep time: 5 minutes Cooking time: 10 minutes Servings: 4 Temperature: HIGH

Ingredients:

- 2 large leeks
- 1 tbsp. olive oil
- 1 tbsp. lime juice
- 2 tbsp. parmesan cheese
- Salt and pepper, as needed

Directions:

1. Trim the rough top green section of the leeks and discard it, then cut the rest into 4-inch sticks and halve them lengthwise. Run them vertiCally under cold water to remove any dirt.
2. Run them vertiCally under cold water to rinse away any dirt. Heat a griddle pan to high heat.
3. Brush the oil on the leeks. Place the sliced side down on a heated griddle pan and cook for a few minutes on each side, or until they begin to brown and soften.
4. Serve with lemon juice, a dusting of parmesan, and salt and pepper to taste.

NUTRITION: Calories: 69, Carbs: 7g, Protein: 2g, Fat: 4g

136. Rosemary Watermelon Steaks

Prep time: 10 minutes
Cooking time: 10 minutes
Servings: 4
Temperature: Medium-High

Ingredients:

- ➢ 1 small watermelon, seeds removed
- ➢ ¼ cup olive oil
- ➢ 1 tbsp. minced fresh rosemary
- ➢ Salt and pepper, as needed.
- ➢ Lemon wedges for serving

Directions:

1. Cut the watermelon into 2-inch-thick slices, with the rind intact, and then into halves or quarters, if you like.
2. Put the oil and rosemary in a small bowl, sprinkle with salt and pepper, and stir. Brush or rub the mixture all over the watermelon slices.
3. Bring the griddle grill to medium-high heat. Oil the griddle and allow it to heat until the oil is shimmering but not smoking.
4. Put the watermelon on the griddle and cook, turning once, until the flesh develops grill marks and has dried out a bit, 4 to 5 minutes per side.
5. Transfer to a platter and serve with lemon wedges.

NUTRITION: Calories: 14, Carbs: 3g, Fat: 0g, Protein: 0g

137. Griddle Wilted Spinach

Prep time: 5 minutes
Cooking time: 1 minute
Servings: 4
Temperature: Medium-High

Ingredients:

- 8 oz. fresh baby spinach
- 1 tbsp. olive oil
- 1/4 tsp garlic powder
- 1/4 tsp salt
- 1 lemon, halved

Directions:

1. Mix the spinach with olive oil, garlic powder, and salt in a mixing bowl.
2. Bring the griddle grill to medium-high heat. Oil the griddle and allow it to heat until the oil is shimmering but not smoking.
3. Lay the spinach in an even layer and grill for 30 seconds. The leaves should wilt but retain just a bit of crunch.
4. Move to a serving bowl and squeeze a bit of lemon juice on top. Serve immediately.

NUTRITION: Calories: 116, Carbs: 5g, Fat: 8g, Protein: 6g

138. Grilled Yellow Potatoes with Paprika

Prep time: 5 minutes
Cooking time: 15 minutes
Servings: 4
Temperature: Medium

Ingredients:

- ➤ 4 small yellow potatoes
- ➤ 1/4 olive oil
- ➤ 1/4 sea salt and black pepper to taste
- ➤ 1/4 paprika

Directions:

1. Cut the potatoes half-lengthwise and put them into a large bag or bowl. Drizzle them with olive oil and stir or shake to coat the potatoes.

2. Add the salt, pepper, and paprika to taste, stir, or shake until completely combined. Pre heat the griddle grill to medium and spray it with oil.

3. Place the potatoes sliced side down, and grill for several minutes or until you can see grill marks and feel tender on the cut side.

4. Turn the potatoes over and grill until they are tender. Remove from heat and serve.

NUTRITION: Calories: 110, Carbs: 26g, Fat: 0g, Protein: 3g

139. Salted Plantains

Prep time: 5 minutes
Cooking time: 10 minutes
Servings: 4
Temperature: Medium-Heat

Ingredients:

- ➢ 2 large ripe plantains, peeled and sliced
- ➢ 2 tbsp. vegetable oil
- ➢ Salt, to taste

Directions:

1. Preheat the griddle to medium heat. Grease the griddle top with cooking spray.
2. Place plantains in a suitable mixing bowl. Season with oil and salt, and then sear on griddle top for 4 minutes per side. Serve.

NUTRITION: Calories 16, Fat 7.1 g, Carbs 28.5g, Protein 1.2g

140. Peppered Butternut Squash

Prep time: 10 minutes
Cooking time: 6 minutes
Servings: 4
Temperature: Medium

Ingredients:

- ➤ 1 small butternut squash (2 pounds), peeled, seeded, and sliced
- ➤ Salt and black pepper to taste
- ➤ 3 tbsp. olive oil

Directions:

1. Add squash slice to a pot filled with boiling water, cook for 3 minutes, and then drain.
2. Preheat the griddle to medium heat. Grease the griddle top with cooking oil.
3. Place squash slices on the hot griddle top and cook 5 minutes per side while seasoning with black pepper and salt. Serve warm.

NUTRITION: Calories 81, Fat 7.1 g, Carbs 5.5g, Protein 0.5g

141. Hawaiian Fried Brown Rice

Prep time: 10 minutes
Cooking time: 10 minutes
Servings: 4
Temperature: Medium-High

Ingredients:

- 3 cups brown rice, cooked
- 1 cup frozen corn
- 2 carrots, peeled and grated
- 1 onion, diced
- Two minced garlic cloves.
- 2 tbsp. extra-virgin olive oil
- 1 tsp powdered ginger
- 1 tbsp. sesame seed oil
- 3 tbsp. Soy sauce
- 1/4 cup finely chopped green onion
- 1/2 cup diced ham
- 2 cups pineapple, diced
- 1 cup frozen peas

Directions:

1. Whisk together the soy sauce, ginger powder, and sesame oil in your small dish. Set aside.
2. Preheat the griddle to medium-high heat. Brush the heated griddle with oil.
3. Cook for 3-4 minutes with the onion and garlic. Add the corn, carrots, and peas and continue to cook for 3-4 minutes.
4. Stir in the cooked rice, green onions, ham, pineapple, and soy sauce mixture for 2- 4 minutes. Arrange on plates and serve.

NUTRITION: Calories: 200, Carbs: 28g, Fat: 70g, Protein: 4g

142. Eggplant with Feta

Prep time: 15 minutes
Cooking time: 25 minutes
Servings: 4
Temperature: Medium-High

Directions:

- ➢ 1 large eggplant, cut into 1/2-inch slices
- ➢ 1 tbsp. salt
- ➢ 3 tbsp. olive oil
- ➢ 4 oz. feta cheese, crumbled
- ➢ 1/2 tsp sweet paprika
- ➢ Freshly ground black pepper
- ➢ 1 lemon, cut in half

Directions:

1. Spread the eggplant slices on a rimmed baking sheet and sprinkle with half of the salt. Flip the slices and sprinkle with the remaining salt.
2. Let sit for 15 minutes to take away some of the bitterness of the eggplant. Transfer the slices to sheets of paper towels and pat dry.
3. Bring the griddle grill to medium-high heat. Oil the griddle and allow it to heat until the oil is shimmering but not smoking.
4. Brush both sides of the eggplant slices with olive oil. Grill for about 6 minutes until the slices have taken on grill marks and are golden brown.
5. Transfer the eggplant to a serving platter and top with the feta, paprika, some pepper, and as quirt of lemon juice. Serve hot or at room temperature.

NUTRITION: Calories: 208, Carbs: 16g, Fat: 16g, Protein: 3g

143. Cheesy Roasted Asparagus

Prep time: 15 minutes
Cooking time: 7 minutes
Servings: 4
Temperature: Medium-High

Ingredients:

- 1 pound medium to thin asparagus, woody stems snapped off and discarded
- 2 tbsp. olive oil
- 1/4 tsp salt
- 1/2 tsp freshly ground black pepper
- 1/4 cup grated Parmesan cheese

Directions:

1. Toss the asparagus, olive oil, salt, plus pepper in a medium bowl.
2. Bring the griddle grill to medium-high heat. Oil the griddle and allow it to heat until the oil is shimmering but not smoke.
3. Grill the asparagus spears for about 7 minutes until they have taken on grill marks and are tender. Sprinkle with parmesan before serving.

NUTRITION: Calories: 226, Carbs: 6g, Fat: 18g, Protein: 10g

144. Griddle Rosemary Polenta

Prep time: 5 minutes
Cooking time: 10 minutes
Servings: 4
Temperature: High

Ingredients:

- ➤ 2/4 oz. prepared polenta log
- ➤ 2 tsp of olive oil
- ➤ garlic salt, to taste
- ➤ lemon pepper, to taste
- ➤ 2 tsp rosemary, chopped

Directions:

1. Preheat the griddle to high heat. Using your sharp knife, cut the polenta into 12- inch-thick pieces. Spread the pieces on your baking sheet.
2. Brush both sides of your polenta rounds with oil and season them with garlic salt, lemon pepper, and rosemary leaves to taste. Lightly oil the grill rack and set it aside.
3. Grill the polenta pieces over high heat for 3 to 5 minutes on each side, or until beautifully browned. Remove and place it on your hot dish to serve.

NUTRITION: Calories 71, Carbs: 16g, Fat 1g, Protein 2g

145. Honey Dijon Cabbage with Thyme

Prep time: 7 minutes
Cooking time: 10 minutes
Servings: 4
Temperature: Medium-High

Ingredients:

- Salt and pepper to taste
- 1 (2-pound) head of green cabbage, cut into 8 wedges through core
- 1 tbsp. minced fresh thyme
- 2 tsp minced shallot
- 2 tsp honey
- 1 tsp Dijon mustard
- ½ tsp grated lemon zest + 2 tbsp. juice
- 6 tbsp. extra-virgin olive oil

Directions:

1. Sprinkle 1-teaspoon salt evenly over cabbage wedges and let them sit within 45 minutes.
2. Combine the thyme, shallot, honey, mustard, lemon zest plus juice, and ¼ teaspoon of pepper in a bowl. Slowly whisk in oil until incorporated. Measure out ¼ cup of the vinaigrette and set it aside.
3. Preheat griddle to medium-high heat and brush with oil.
4. Brush 1 cut side of your cabbage wedges with half of the vinaigrette. Place cabbage on your griddle, vinaigrette side down, and cook until well browned, within 7 to 10 minutes.
5. Brush the tops of wedges with the rest of the vinaigrette: flip and cook until the second side is well browned and fork-tender, within 7 to 10 minutes.
6. Transfer cabbage to your platter and drizzle with the reserved vinaigrette. Season with salt, plus pepper to taste. Serve.

NUTRITION: Calories: 71, Carbs: 9g, Fat: 4g, Protein: 2g

146. Broccoli Rice with Tomatillos & Cilantro

Prep time: 7 minutes
Cooking time: 40 minutes
Servings: 4
Temperature: High

Ingredients:

- 6 large tomatillos, peeled and rinsed
- Oil, for coating
- 1 white onion, coarsely chopped
- 2 cups cilantro (leaves and stems)
- 1 tbsp. roasted garlic
- 2 tsp salt, plus more for seasoning
- 1½ cups water
- 2 cups white rice
- 1 bunch sCallions, bases trimmed
- 1 head of broccoli, cut in half
- 1 cup basil leaves, coarsely chopped
- 1 cup parsley leaves, coarsely chopped

Directions:

1. Preheat griddle to high heat and brush with oil.

2. Toss the tomatillos in enough oil to coat and cook over high heat until charred, about 5 minutes, often turning to char evenly.

3. Transfer to a blender with the onion, 1 cup of the cilantro, the garlic, salt, and water, and puree until smooth. Set aside.

4. Add the rice, then cook, constantly stirring, until toasted and slightly translucent, about 3 minutes.

5. Pour in the tomatillo puree and stir to combine. Cook, stirring only if necessary to avoid burning, until most of the liquid has been absorbed, 10 to 12 minutes.

6. Cover and cook for 5 more minutes. Keeping the lid on, remove it from the griddle and let it sit and steam until ready to serve.

7. While the rice cooks, toss the sCallions and broccoli in enough oil to coat.

8. Cook over medium heat until charred but not burned, about 1 minute for the sCallions and 5minutes for the broccoli (lay the sCallions crosswise on the griddle).

9. Remove from the griddle, place both in a bowl, tightly cover, and let steam for 5 to 10 minutes.

10. Coarsely chop the sCallions, broccoli, and the remaining 1-cup of cilantro. Add to the rice together with the basil and parsley. Fluff with a fork, season with salt and serve immediately.

NUTRITION: Calories: 200, Carbs: 33g, Fat: 3g, Protein: 10g

147. Cheesy Baby Potatoes

Prep time: 10 minutes
Cooking time: 25-30 minutes
Servings: 4
Temperature: Medium

Ingredients:

➢ 1 1/2 lb. baby potatoes, pierced 2 times

➢ 2 tbsp. olive oil + more as needed

➢ 2 tbsp. butter, dissolved

➢ 2 tbsp. parmesan cheese

➢ 1 tbsp. favorite seasoning

➢ 1 tbsp. parsley flat-leaf, chopped butter, as needed

Directions:

1. Place the baby potatoes in your skillet with enough water and boiled until tender.

2. Brush your potatoes with olive oil and cover using your plastic wrap until you are ready to smash on your griddle.

3. Combine the olive oil, butter, cheese, seasoning, and parsley in your small mixing bowl.

4. Preheat the griddle to medium heat, swirl some butter around your griddle, and place the baby potatoes.

5. Smash the baby potatoes down using your spatula and burger press. Drizzle it with the cheese plus herb mixture, and let it cook until crisp and golden brown.

NUTRITION: Calories: 120, Carbs: 14g, Fat: 5g, Protein: 7g

148. Bacon Green Beans with Maple Glazed

Prep time: 15 minutes
Cooking time: 10 minutes
Servings: 4
Temperature: Medium

Ingredients:

- 1 (12 oz.) bag of frozen green beans
- 6 oz.. package of bacon
- 1/2 cup of diced onion
- Pure maple syrup, as needed
- Black pepper and salt to taste

Directions:

1. Grease the cooking surface of the griddle with cooking spray. Warm your griddle to medium heat.
2. Slice the bacon into small strips, add to the griddle top, and cook until crispy.
3. Add beans to the other side of your griddle and season with black pepper and salt to taste.
4. Add the onions and sauté them in the bacon grease when the bacon is nearly done.
5. After 2 minutes, combine all of the
6. Ingredients in the recipe, allowing the bacon grease to flavor everything. Serve.

NUTRITION: Calories 392: Fat 31g: Carbs 16g: Protein 28g

149. Griddle Leeks

Prep time: 5 minutes
Cooking time: 14 minutes
Servings: 4
Temperature: Medium-Low

Ingredients:

- 4 leeks (1-1 ½ pounds)
- salt and pepper, as needed
- olive oil, as needed

Directions:

1. Preheat a griddle to medium-low heat. Trim the stiff green tips and root ends of your leeks.
2. Cut a large vertiCal slit through the middle of the leek from the root end to the remaining green section, but do not cut through.
3. Rinse well to remove the sand from between the layers. Season both sides with salt.
4. Cut the leeks in half, place them straight on the grill, cut side down, and push lightly with a spatula to ensure the layers spread out over the fire.
5. Cook for 6 to 8 minutes, depending on their thickness, until softened. Brush with oil, flip, and cook for 1 to 3 minutes
6. Until the bottom is browned.
7. Brush the top with oil, flip, and cook for 1 to 3 minutes. Serve the leeks hot, heated, or at room temperature with a sprinkling of pepper.

NUTRITION: Calories 63, Carbs 9g, Fat 3g, Protein 1g

150. Parmesan Tomatoes with Rosemary

Prep time: 10 minutes
Cooking time: 20 minutes
Servings: 6
Temperature: Medium

Ingredients:

- ➢ 1/2 tsp ground black pepper
- ➢ 1 tbsp. dried rosemary
- ➢ 9 halved tomatoes
- ➢ 5 minced garlic cloves
- ➢ 1 cup grated Parmesan cheese
- ➢ 1/4 tsp onion powder
- ➢ 1 tsp kosher salt
- ➢ 2 tbsp. olive oil

Directions:

1. Preheat your griddle at medium heat and apply a thin layer of oil on top of the griddle.
2. Cook for around 5-7 minutes with the sliced side of the tomatoes down on the griddle.
3. In a medium-sized pan, heat the olive oil on the griddle. Cook for around 3-5 minutes with the garlic, onion powder, rosemary, black pepper, and salt.
4. Remove the pan from the griddle and set it aside. Brush each tomato half with the olive oil garlic combination and sprinkle with grated parmesan cheese before serving.
5. Close the griddle and continue to cook for another 7-10minutes, or till the cheese has melted. Remove the tomatoes from the griddle & serve immediately.

NUTRITION: Calories 130, Fat 8g, Protein 6g, Carbs 9g

151. Green Onion Rice

Prep time: 10 minutes
Cooking time: 10 minutes
Servings: 4
Temperature: High

Ingredients:

- 4 cups rice, cooked
- 2 large eggs
- 2 tbsp. green onion, sliced
- 2 tbsp. olive oil
- 1 tsp salt

Directions:

1. In a bowl, whisk eggs and set aside.
2. Preheat the griddle to high heat. Spray griddle top with cooking spray.
3. Add cooked rice to the hot griddle top and fry until rice separates from each other. Push rice to one side of the griddle top. Add oil to the griddle and pour a beaten egg.
4. Add salt and mix egg quickly with rice and cook until rice grains are covered by egg. Put the green onion and stir fry for 2 minutes. Serve and enjoy.

NUTRITION: Calories: 75, Carbs: 14g, Fat: 2g, Protein: 2g

152. Griddle Plum-Tomatoes

Prep time: 5 minutes
Cooking time: 60 minutes
Servings: 4
Temperature: Medium-Low

Ingredients:

➢ 4 plum tomatoes, cut half lengthwise

➢ olive oil, as needed

➢ salt and pepper, as needed

Directions:

1. Preheat an indirect griddle over medium-low heat. Brush the tomatoes with oil, then season with salt plus pepper on both sides.

2. Place the tomatoes, cut side up, on the indirect side of the grill. To prevent charring, keep the tomatoes away from the heat if the temperature is closer to medium.

3. Close the grill and cook until the vegetables are shriveled but still show traces of moisture, at least 1 hour and up to 3 hours.

4. About halfway through, move and rotate the tomatoes to ensure equal cooking. Transfer to your serving dish and serve right away.

NUTRITION: Calories 100, Carbs: 16g, Fat 1, Protein 5g

153. Stir Fry Cabbage

Prep time: 5 minutes
Cooking time: 5 minutes
Servings: 4
Temperature: High

Ingredients:

- 1 cabbage head, tear cabbage leaves, washed and drained
- 2 green onions, sliced
- 1 tbsp. ginger, minced
- 2 garlic cloves, minced
- 1 tbsp. soy sauce
- 1/2 tbsp. vinegar
- 4 dried chilies
- 2 tbsp. olive oil
- 1/2 tsp salt

Directions:

1. Preheat the griddle to high heat, and add oil to the hot griddle top.
2. Add ginger, garlic, green onion and sauté for 2-3 minutes. Add dried chilies and sauté for 30seconds.
3. Add cabbage, vinegar, soy sauce, and salt and stir-fry for 1-2 minutes over high heat until cabbage wilted. Serve and enjoy.

NUTRITION: Calories: 115, Fat: 7.3 g, Carbs: 12.7 g, Protein: 2.9 g

154. Crisp Baby Artichokes with Lemon Aioli

Prep time: 15 minutes
Cooking time: 10 minutes
Servings: 4
Temperature: Medium-High

Ingredients:

- 2 tbsp. olive oil
- Grated zest and juice of 1 lemon
- 8 baby artichokes
- 1/2 cup mayonnaise
- 1 tsp minced garlic, or more to taste
- Salt and pepper, as needed

Directions:

1. Whisk the oil and lemon juice in a large bowl. Peel away and discard the outer layers of each artichoke until the leaves are half-yellow and half-green.
2. Cut across the top of the artichoke with a sharp knife to remove the green tops. Leave 1inch of stem and use a paring knife or vegetable peeler to trim the bottom so no green remains.
3. Cut the artichoke in half lengthwise from top to bottom. As each artichoke is trimmed, add it to the olive oil mixture and toss to coat evenly: this helps delay discoloring.
4. Put the mayonnaise, garlic, and lemon zest in a small bowl, sprinkle with salt and pepper, and whisk to combine. Taste and adjust the seasoning.
5. Bring the griddle grill to medium-high heat. Oil the griddle and allow it to heat until the oil is shimmering but not smoke.
6. Put the artichokes cut side down on the grill and cook until tender and charred, 8 to 10 Minutes. Transfer to a plate and serve with the aioli for dipping.

NUTRITION: Calories: 122, Fat: 8.2g, Carbs: 9.5g, Protein: 1g

155. Tomato Melts with Spinach Salad

Prep time: 5 minutes
Cooking time: 10 minutes
Servings: 4
Temperature: Medium-High

Ingredients:

- 1 or 2 large fresh tomatoes (enough for 4 thick slices across)
- 2 tbsp. good-quality olive oil, plus more for brushing
- Salt and pepper, as needed
- 2 tsp white wine vinegar
- 1 tsp Dijon mustard
- 3 cups baby spinach
- 6 slices of cheddar cheese

Directions:

1. Core the tomatoes and cut four thick slices (about 1 inch): save the trimmings. Brush them with oil, then sprinkle with salt plus pepper on both sides.
2. Whisk the 2 tablespoons of oil, vinegar, and mustard together in a bowl. Chop the trimmings from the tomatoes: add them to the dressing along with the spinach, and toss until evenly coated.
3. Bring the griddle grill to medium-high heat. Oil the griddle and allow it to heat until the oil is shimmering but not smoke.
4. Put the tomato slices and cook for 3 minutes. Turn the tomatoes, top each slice with a slice of cheddar, and cook until the cheese is melted 2 to 3 minutes.
5. Transfer to plates and serve with the salad on top.

NUTRITION: Calories: 218, Fat: 12.8 g, Carbs: 25.2 g, Protein: 2.8 g

156. Parmesan Broccoli Grill-Fry

Prep time: 15 minutes
Cooking time: 5 minutes
Servings: 4
Temperature: Medium

Ingredients:

- 4 tbsp. olive oil
- 1 tsp minced garlic
- 6 cups broccoli florets
- Salt to taste
- 2 tbsp. fresh lemon juice
- ½ cup grated parmesan cheese

Directions:

1. Preheat the griddle to medium heat and add the oil.
2. Sauté the garlic for 30 seconds before adding the broccoli florets—season with salt and lemon juice.
3. Stir for 5 minutes before adding the parmesan cheese. Serve and enjoy!

NUTRITION: Calories: 228: Protein: 8 g: Carbs: 14 g: Fat: 17 g

157. Zucchini Antipasto

Prep time: 10 minutes
Cooking time: 6 minutes
Servings: 4
Temperature: Medium-High

Ingredients:

- ¼ cup olive oil
- 3 garlic cloves, minced
- 1 tbsp. fresh thyme leaves or ½ tsp dried thyme
- ¼ tsp salt
- ¼ tsp freshly ground black pepper
- 4 medium zucchinis, cut lengthwise into ¼-inch-thick slices
- 1 tbsp. balsamic vinegar

Directions:

1. Whisk the olive oil, garlic, thyme, salt, and pepper in a large bowl. Add the zucchini and toss to coat.
2. Bring the griddle grill to medium-high heat. Oil the griddle and allow it to heat until the oil is shimmering but not smoke.
3. Grill for about 6 minutes until the zucchini slices have taken on grill marks and are very tender. Serve either hot off the grill or sprinkled with the vinegar at room temperature.

NUTRITION: Calories: 156: Carbs: 8g: Fat: 14g: Protein: 2g

158. Grilled Mushrooms with Rosemary

Prep time: 5 minutes
Cooking time: 20 minutes
Servings: 4
Temperature: Medium

Ingredients:

- ➢ 4 large Porto bello mushrooms, or 1½ pounds shiitake, button, or creamy mushrooms
- ➢ 1/3 cup olive oil
- ➢ 1 tbsp. minced shallot, sCallion, onion, or garlic
- ➢ 1 tbsp. chopped fresh rosemary
- ➢ Salt and pepper, as needed

Directions:

1. Heat a griddle for medium heat. Rinse and trim the mushrooms to remove any tough stems. Combine the oil, shallot, rosemary, and some salt and pepper in a small bowl.
2. Brush your mushrooms all over with about half of the mixture: reserve the rest. Skewer the mushrooms if they are small or place them in a perforated grill pan.
3. Place the mushrooms on the grill directly. Cook while turning or shaking the pan to cook evenly until they soften and a knife pierces the center with no resistance, within 5 to 20 minutes.
4. Brush with the remaining oil as they cook. Transfer to a platter, and serve!

NUTRITION: Calories: 87, Carbs: 8g, Fat: 3g, Protein: 7g

159. Tofu Steaks

Prep time: 10 minutes
Cooking time: 10 minutes
Servings: 4
Temperature: High

Ingredients:

- 1 (14-16 oz.) block of firm tofu
- olive oil for brushing
- Salt, as needed
- Pepper, as needed (optional)

Directions:

1. Cut the tofu across into 1-inch-thick steaks. Pat dry using your paper towels, brush with oil, and sprinkle with salt on both sides.
2. Bring the griddle grill to high heat, and oil the griddle. Put the tofu on your grill and cook, turning once, until the slices develop a crust and release easily from the grate, about 5 minutes per side.
3. Sprinkle with more salt plus pepper if you like, and serve.

NUTRITION: Calories: 160, Carbs: 14g, Fat: 2g, Protein: 12g

160. Butternut Squash with Melted Butter

Prep time: 5 minutes
Cooking time: 60 minutes
Servings: 4
Temperature: Medium-High

Ingredients:

- ➤ 2 pounds butternut squash, cut into large pieces and seeded
- ➤ 4 tbsp. (½ stick) butter, melted
- ➤ Salt and pepper, as needed

Directions:

1. Heat a griddle for medium-high heat. Brush the cut sides of your squash with about half of the melted butter, then sprinkle with salt and pepper.
2. Place the squash on the grill directly, skin side down. Cook until a skewer can be inserted through the center of each chunk without resistance, about 1 hour depending on their thickness.
3. Transfer to a cutting board. Slice the blackened skin, and then cut the squash into bite- sized cubes.
4. Place in a serving bowl and spry with the remaining melted butter. Taste and adjust the seasoning, toss to combine, and serve.

NUTRITION: Calories: 272, Carbs: 71g, Fat: 1g, Protein: 6g

161. Grilled Corn with Paprika

Prep time: 15 minutes
Cooking time: 6 minutes
Servings: 4
Temperature: Medium

Ingredients:

- ➢ 4 ears of corn, husked
- ➢ 1 tbsp. melted salted butter
- ➢ 1 tsp Spanish paprika

Directions:

1. Preheat the griddle to medium heat and add the oil—Grill the corn for 3 minutes on each side.
2. Once cooked, brush with salted butter and sprinkle with paprika.

NUTRITION: Calories: 141: Protein: 5 g: Carbs: 28 g: Sugar: 14 g: Fat: 4 g

162. Griddled Summer Vegetables

Prep time: 15 minutes
Cooking time: 6 minutes
Servings: 4
Temperature: Medium

Ingredients:

- ➢ 1 tbsp. olive oil
- ➢ 1 cup asparagus spears, cleaned
- ➢ 1 large eggplant, sliced
- ➢ 1 zucchini, sliced
- ➢ 1 fennel bulb, sliced
- ➢ Juice from ½ lemon
- ➢ Salt and pepper to taste

Directions:

1. Heat the griddle pan to medium and brush with oil. Place the vegetables on the griddle pan.

2. Season with lemon juice, salt, and pepper. Cook until the vegetables are roasted.

NUTRITION: Calories: 95: Protein: 3 g: Carbs: 15 g: Fat: 4 g

163. Cauliflower with Garlic and Anchovies

Prep time: 5 minutes
Cooking time: 20 minutes
Servings: 4
Temperature: Medium-High

Ingredients:

- 1 head cauliflower (11/2-2 pounds)
- 6 table tbsp. olive oil
- 6 oil-packed anchovy fillets, chopped, or more to taste
- 1 tbsp. minced garlic
- 1/2 tsp red chile flakes, or as needed
- Salt and pepper (optional)
- Chopped fresh parsley for garnish (optional)

Directions:

1. Break or cut the cauliflower into florets about 11/2 inches across: put in a bowl.
2. Put the oil, anchovies, garlic, and red pepper if using it in a small skillet over medium-low heat.
3. Cook, often stirring, until the anchovies break up and the garlic just begins to color about 5minutes.
4. Taste and add more anchovies or some salt and pepper. Pour half of the oil mixture over the cauliflower: toss to coat evenly with it.
5. Bring the griddle grill to medium-high heat. Oil the griddle and allow it to heat until the oil is shimmering but not smoke.
6. Put the florets in a single and cook until the cauliflower is as tender and browned as you like it, 5 minutes for crisp-tender to 10 minutes for fully tender.
7. Transfer to a serving bowl, drizzle over the remaining sauce and the parsley, toss gently and serve warm or at room temperature.

NUTRITION: Calories: 100, Fat: 5 g, Carbs: 11.7 g, Protein: 3.1 g

164. Seared Sesame Green Beans

Prep time: 10 minutes
Cooking time: 10 minutes
Servings: 4
Temperature: Medium-High

Ingredients:

- ➢ 1 ½ pound of trimmed green beans
- ➢ 1 ½ tsp rice vinegar
- ➢ 3 tbsp. soy sauce
- ➢ 1 ½ tsp sesame oil
- ➢ 2 tbsp. roasted sesame seeds
- ➢ 1 ½ tbsp. brown sugar
- ➢ ¼ tsp ground black pepper

Directions:

1. Cook your green beans in a skillet with boiling water for 3 minutes, then drain thoroughly. Drain the green beans, place them in a bowl of ice water, and pat dry using your paper towel.
2. Preheat the griddle to medium-high heat. Brush the heated griddle with oil.
3. Stir in the green beans for 2 minutes. Add the soy sauce, brown sugar, vinegar, and pepper and cook within 2 minutes.
4. Toss in your sesame seeds to coat them. Arrange on plates and serve.

NUTRITION: Calories: 100, Fat: 3.9g, Carbs :11.7g, Protein: 3.1g

165. Coleslaw with Cilantro

Prep time: 10 minutes
Cooking time: 15 minutes
Servings: 4
Temperature: Medium

Ingredients:

- ½ (1-pound) head of green cabbage, cut into wedges
- 1 carrot, peeled and shredded
- 2 tbsp. minced fresh cilantro
- 2 tbsp. olive oil
- ¼ cup mayonnaise
- 1 shallot, minced
- 4 tsp cider vinegar
- Salt and black pepper to taste

Directions:

1. Preheat the griddle to medium heat. Grease the griddle top with cooking oil.
2. Season the cabbage wedges with salt and black pepper after brushing them with oil.
3. Arrange the cabbage on the hot griddle top. Cook for 12 minutes until browned. Place cabbage on a plate and cover with aluminum foil to keep it warm.
4. In a suitable mixing bowl, mix shallot, mayonnaise, and vinegar. Remove the core from the cabbage and slice it into thin strips.
5. Mix the carrot, cabbage, salt, black pepper, and cilantro with the mayonnaise until well combined. Serve and enjoy.

NUTRITION: Calories 149, Fat 12 g, Carbs 10.5g, Protein 1.5g

166. Cabbage Carrot Grilled Tempeh

Prep time: 5 minutes
Cooking time: 6 minutes
Servings: 4
Temperature: High

Ingredients:

- ➢ 1 (8-ounce) piece of tempeh
- ➢ olive oil for brushing
- ➢ Salt, as needed
- ➢ Pepper, as needed (optional)

Directions:

1. Brush the tempeh with oil and sprinkle with salt on both sides.
2. Bring the griddle grill to high heat. Oil the griddle. Put the tempeh and cook until it develops a crust and releases easily from the grates, about 6 minutes.
3. Sprinkle with more salt plus pepper if you like, and serve.

NUTRITION: Calories: 193. Carbs: 9g, Fat: 11g, Protein: 19g

167. Stir Fry Zucchini & Carrots

Prep time: 10 minutes
Cooking time: 10 minutes
Servings: 4
Temperature: High

Ingredients:

- 2 zucchinis, sliced
- 1 tsp garlic powder
- 1 tsp dried parsley
- 1 tsp dried thyme
- 3 carrots, sliced
- 2 tbsp. olive oil
- ½ tsp dried oregano
- Salt and pepper to taste
- Cooking spray

Directions:

1. Add zucchini, carrots, and the remaining
2. Ingredients into the mixing bowl and toss well.
3. Preheat the griddle to high heat. Spray the griddle top with cooking spray.
4. Place the zucchini and carrot mixture on the hot griddle top and cook for 8-10 minutes. Serve and enjoy.

NUTRITION: Calories: 98, Fat: 7.2 g, Carbs: 8.6 g, Protein: 1.7 g

168. Bok Choy Stir-Fry

Prep time: 10 minutes
Cooking time: 5 minutes
Servings: 4
Temperature: Medium-High

Ingredients:

- ➢ 2 Bok choy heads, trimmed and sliced crosswise
- ➢ 1 tbsp. sesame oil
- ➢ 2 tbsp. soy sauce
- ➢ 2 tsp water
- ➢ 1 tbsp. melted butter
- ➢ 1 tsp peanut oil
- ➢ 1 tsp oyster sauce
- ➢ 1/2 tsp salt

Directions:

1. In y our small bowl, combine soy sauce, oyster sauce, sesame oil, and water: set aside.
2. Preheat the griddle to medium-high heat. Brush the heated griddle with oil.
3. Stir in the Bok Choy and salt for 2 minutes. Stir in the butter and soy sauce mixture. Arrange on plates and serve.

NUTRITION: Calories: 67, Carbs: 6g, Fat: 4g, Protein: 3g

169. Balsamic Mushroom Skewers

Prep time: 10 minutes
Cooking time: 10 minutes
Servings: 4
Temperature: Medium-High

Ingredients:

- 2 lb. sliced ¼-inch thick mushrooms
- 1/2 tsp chopped thyme
- 3 chopped garlic cloves
- 1 tbsp. soy sauce
- 2 tbsp. balsamic vinegar
- pepper and salt to taste

Directions:

1. Add mushrooms and remaining
2. Ingredients into the mixing bowl, cover, and place in the refrigerator for 30 minutes.
3. Thread marinated mushrooms onto the skewers. Heat the griddle to medium-high heat. Place mushroom skewers onto the hot griddle and cook for 2-3 minutes per side. Serve.

NUTRITION: Calories: 60, Fat: 1g, Carbs: 8g, Protein: 6g

170. Balsamic Mushroom Skewers

Prep time: 10 minutes
Cooking time: 10 minutes
Servings: 4
Temperature: Medium-High

Ingredients:

- ➢ 2 pounds Yukon Gold potatoes, unpeeled
- ➢ 1 tbsp. olive oil
- ➢ 2 garlic cloves, peeled and chopped
- ➢ 1 tsp minced fresh thyme
- ➢ 1 tsp salt
- ➢ ½ tsp pepper

Directions:

1. Cut each potato in half crosswise, then cut each half into 8 wedges.
2. Place potatoes in a large bowl, cover, and microwave until the edges of potatoes are translucent, 4 to 7 minutes, shaking the bowl to redistribute potatoes halfway through microwaving. Drain well.
3. Gently toss potatoes with oil, garlic, thyme, salt, and pepper.
4. Cut four 14 by 10-inch sheets of heavy-duty aluminum foil. Working one at a time, spread one-quarter of the potato mixture over half of the foil, fold the foil over potatoes, and crimp edges tightly to seal.
5. Preheat griddle to medium-high heat and brush with oil.
6. Place hobo packs on the griddle and cook, covered, until potatoes are completely tender, about 10 minutes, flipping packs halfway through cooking. Cut open foil and serve.

NUTRITION: Calories: 337, Carbs: 27g, Fat: 13g, Protein: 31g

171. Potato Hobo Packs

Prep time: 16 minutes
Cooking time: 30 minutes
Servings: 4
Temperature: Medium-High

Ingredients:

- ➤ 2 pounds Yukon Gold potatoes, unpeeled
- ➤ 1 tbsp. olive oil
- ➤ 2 garlic cloves, peeled and chopped
- ➤ 1 tsp minced fresh thyme
- ➤ 1 tsp salt
- ➤ ½ tsp pepper

Directions:

2. Cut each potato in half crosswise, then cut each half into 8 wedges.
3. Place potatoes in a large bowl, cover, and microwave until the edges of potatoes are translucent, 4 to 7 minutes, shaking the bowl to redistribute potatoes halfway through microwaving. Drain well.
4. Gently toss potatoes with oil, garlic, thyme, salt, and pepper.
5. Cut four 14 by 10-inch sheets of heavy-duty aluminum foil. Working one at a time, spread one-quarter of the potato mixture over half of the foil, fold the foil over potatoes, and crimp edges tightly to seal.
6. Preheat griddle to medium-high heat and brush with oil.
7. Place hobo packs on the griddle and cook, covered, until potatoes are completely tender, about 10 minutes, flipping packs halfway through cooking. Cut open foil and serve.

NUTRITION: Calories: 337, Carbs: 27g, Fat: 13g, Protein: 31g

172. Sautéed Vegetables

Prep time: 10 minutes
Cooking time: 5 minutes
Servings: 4
Temperature: Medium-High

Ingredients:

- ➢ 2 medium zucchini matchsticks
- ➢ 2 tsp coconut oil
- ➢ 2 tsp minced garlic
- ➢ 1 tsp honey
- ➢ 3 tbsp. Soy sauce
- ➢ 1 tsp sesame seeds
- ➢ 2 cups of carrots, shaved into matchsticks
- ➢ 2 cups thawed snow peas

Directions:

1. In your small bowl, combine the soy sauce, garlic, and honey: set aside.
2. Preheat the griddle to medium-high heat. Brush the heated griddle with oil.
3. Sauté the carrots, peas, and zucchini for 1-2 minutes. Stir in the soy sauce mixture for 1minute. Garnish with sesame seeds before serving.

NUTRITION: Calories 160, Fat 12.1g, Carbs 7.5g, Protein 5.3g

173. Stir Fry Mushrooms with Thyme

Prep time: 15 minutes
Cooking time: 15 minutes
Servings: 4
Temperature: High

Ingredients:

- ➢ 10 oz. mushrooms, sliced
- ➢ 1/4 cup olive oil
- ➢ 1 tbsp. garlic, minced
- ➢ 1/4 tsp dried thyme
- ➢ Pepper, as needed
- ➢ Salt, as needed

Directions:

1. Preheat the griddle to high heat. Add 2 tablespoons of oil to the hot griddle top.
1. 2. Add mushrooms, garlic, thyme, pepper, salt, and sauté mushrooms until tender– drizzle   remaining oil and serve.

NUTRITION: Calories: 253, Fat: 25.6 g, Carbs: 6.2 g, Protein: 4.7 g

174. Egg Plant with Yogurt

Prep time: 10 minutes
Cooking time: 30 minutes
Servings: 4
Temperature: Medium-High

Directions:

- ➢ 6 tablespoons extra-virgin olive oil
- ➢ 5 garlic cloves, minced
- ➢ 1/8 tsp red pepper flakes
- ➢ ½ cup plain whole-milk yogurt
- ➢ 3 tbsp. minced fresh mint
- ➢ 1 tsp grated lemon zest + 2 tsp juice
- ➢ 1 tsp ground cumin
- ➢ Salt and pepper to taste
- ➢ 2 pounds eggplant, sliced into ¼-inch-thick rounds

Directions:

1. Microwave the oil, garlic, plus pepper flakes in your bowl until garlic is golden and crisp, within 2 minutes.
2. Strain the oil through your fine mesh strainer into a clean bowl: reserve the oil and crispy garlic mixture separately.
3. Combine 1 tbsp. strained garlic oil, yogurt, mint, lemon zest plus juice, cumin, and
2. ¼ tsp salt in your bowl: set aside.
3. Brush the eggplant thoroughly with remaining garlic oil and season with salt plus pepper.
4. Preheat your griddle to medium-high heat. Clean and oil your griddle. Place half of the eggplant on your griddle and cook, often turning, until browned and tender, within 8 to 10minutes.
5. Transfer to your platter and repeat with the remaining eggplant. Before serving, drizzle with yogurt sauce and sprinkle with crispy garlic mixture.

NUTRITION: Calories: 210, Carbs: 14g, Fat: 17g, Protein: 3g

175. Creamy Grilled Potato Salad

Prep time: 15 minutes
Cooking time: 10 minutes
Servings: 4
Temperature: Medium-High

Ingredients:

- 1 (1 lb.) bag of baby white potatoes

For the dressing:

- 2 tsp apple cider vinegar
- 1 tsp celery seed
- 1 tbsp. lemon juice
- ½ tsp sea salt
- ½ cup mayonnaise
- 1 tbsp. fresh parsley, chopped
- 1 tbsp. sour cream
- 2 tbsp. olive oil
- 1 tbsp. fresh basil, chopped
- 1 tbsp. Dijon mustard
- ½ tsp black pepper

Directions:

1. Apply the thin layer of olive oil to the griddle and preheat at medium-high temperature. Place potatoes on the griddle and heat for 10 minutes or until tender.
2. Remove the potatoes from the griddle and set them aside for 10 minutes to cool.
3. In a large-sized mixing bowl, whisk together the dressing
4. Ingredients until well blended.
5. Fold in the potatoes until thoroughly combined, then serve at room temperature or chilled overnight.

NUTRITION: Calories 132, Fat 9g, Protein 2g, Carbs 14g

176. Grilled Okra

Prep time: 5 minutes
Cooking time: 5 minutes
Servings: 4
Temperature: Medium

Ingredients:

- ➢ 1 1/2 pounds okra pods, stem ends trimmed
- ➢ 2 tbsp. olive oil
- ➢ 2 tsp coarse sea salt

Directions:

1. Heat a griddle for medium heat. Place the okra in a bowl. Spray with the oil and toss to coat completely. Sprinkle with the salt and toss again.
2. Place the okra on the grill directly. Cook it while turning them once or twice until the pods turn bright green within 5 to 10 minutes. Transfer to your platter and serve hot.

NUTRITION: Calories: 27, Carbs: 6g, Fat: 0g, Protein: 2g

177. Steamed Ranch Carrots

Prep time: 15 minutes Cooking
time: 20 minutes Servings: 4
Temperature: MEDIUM

Ingredients:

- ➤ 12 petite carrots
- ➤ 1 packet dry ranch dressing/seasoning mix
- ➤ 2 olive oil
- ➤ Water, as needed

Directions:

1. Grease the cooking surface of the griddle with cooking spray, and preheat to medium heat.
2. Combine carrots, olive oil, and ranch seasoning mix in a suitable bowl, and stir until well combined.
3. Add carrots to the griddle and then let it cook for almost 3 minutes, with occasional stirring. Add 3 tablespoons of water to your pile of carrots to generate steam.
4. Cover the carrot pile with a basting cover. Toss carrots, add 2-3 tablespoons of water and re-cover with basting marinade to continue steaming.
5. Cook the carrots within 12 minutes or to desired tenderness. Serve.

NUTRITION: Calories 304: Fat 14.9g: Carbs 12g: Protein 21g

178. Griddle Buttered Radish

Prep time: 5 minutes
Cooking time: 6 minutes
Servings: 4
Temperature: Medium-High

Ingredients:

- ➤ 1-pound whole radishes, with greens attached
- ➤ 2 tbsp. olive oil
- ➤ 8 tbsp. (1 stick) butter, softened
- ➤ 1 to 2 tbsp. sea salt

Directions:

1. Trim the root ends, then remove any discolored leaves from the radishes. Rinse, pat them dry using your paper towels, and toss with the oil until completely coated, including the greens.
2. Bring the griddle grill to medium-high heat. Oil the griddle and allow it to heat until the oil is shimmering but not smoke.
3. Put the radishes on the grill, and cook until they warm through and char in places, 4 to 6minutes. Transfer to your platter and serve with the butter and salt in small bowls for dipping.

NUTRITION: Calories: 65, Carbs: 3g, Fat: 2g, Protein: 0g

179. Citrus Fennel Salad

Prep time: 10 minutes
Cooking time: 10 minutes
Servings: 4
Temperature: Medium

Ingredients:

- ½ cup rice vinegar
- ¼ cup sugar
- 1 small red onion, halved, thinly sliced, and pulled apart
- 2 pounds fennel
- 2 tbsp. olive oil, + more for brushing
- 3 navel oranges
- 1 tsp minced fresh rosemary
- Salt and pepper, as needed

Directions:

1. Put the vinegar plus sugar in a small nonreactive saucepan and bring to a boil. Remove, then put the onion, and mix to combine.
2. Heat your griddle to medium heat.
3. Trim the fennel bulbs, reserving the feathery fronds. Cut the fennel in half from stalk end to base: brush with oil.
4. Cut the peel from your oranges with a small knife, deep enough to remove the white pith. Slice the oranges into ¼-inch rounds, cut the rounds into wedges, and place them in a large bowl.
5. Place the fennel on the grill directly. Turn once until the fennel is crisp-tender and brown edor charred in spots, 3 to 5 minutes per side.
6. Transfer it to a cutting board and thinly slice it across into crescents. Add to the oranges.
7. Use a slotted spoon to transfer the onion to the bowl: reserve the brine. Mince enough fennel fronds to make 2 tablespoons.
8. Add the oil, 1 tablespoon of the brine, the rosemary, the minced fronds, and some salt and pepper. Toss to coat, taste and adjust the seasoning, and serve.

NUTRITION: Calories: 113, Carbs: 23g, Fat: 0g, Protein: 2g

180. Garlic Lemon Mushrooms

Prep time: 10 minutes
Cooking time: 13 minutes
Servings: 4
Temperature: Medium

Ingredients:

- ½ cup olive oil
- 3 tbsp. lemon juice
- 6 garlic cloves, minced
- ¼ tsp salt
- 4 Portobello mushrooms (6 inches in diameter), stemmed

Directions:

1. Mix the lemon juice, oil, garlic, and salt in a Zip lock bag. Toss in the mushrooms, seal the bag, shake well and marinate for 30 minutes.
2. Preheat the griddle to medium heat. Grease the griddle top with cooking spray.
3. Pour the egg mixture onto the hot griddle top. Cut four 12-inch squares of an aluminum foil sheet.
4. Remove the mushrooms from the marinade and lay them on a foil square. Seal the edges of the foil around each mushroom.
5. Place foil packets on griddle top sealed side up, and cook for 12 minutes. Unwrap mushrooms with tongs and set them on the griddle for 60 seconds. Serve.

NUTRITION: Calories 164, Fat 16.9 g, Carbs 3.2g, Protein 2.3g

181. Bacon-Wrapped Asparagus

Prep time: 15 minutes
Cooking time: 25 minutes
Servings: 4
Temperature: High

Ingredients:

- 15 to 20 fresh asparagus spears
- olive oil, as needed
- 5 bacon slices, thinly sliced
- 1 tsp salt
- 1 tsp pepper

Directions:

1. Break off the ends of the asparagus, then trim them all to the same length. Separate the asparagus into bundles of three spears each.
2. Spritz some olive oil over them. Wrap each bundle with a slice of your bacon. Sprinkle the wrapped bundle with salt and pepper.
3. Preheat the griddle to high heat. Griddle the wraps for 25 to 30 minutes, depending on the size. Serve!

NUTRITION: Calories 71, Fat 3g, Carbs 1g, Protein 6g

182. Garlic Bell Peppers with Sherry Vinegar

Prep time: 20 minutes
Cooking time: 35 minutes
Servings: 4
Temperature: MEDIUM

Ingredients:

- ¼ cup olive oil
- 3 garlic cloves, peeled and smashed
- Salt and black pepper to taste
- 6 red bell peppers
- 1 tbsp. sherry vinegar

Directions:

1. Mix the garlic, oil, ¼-teaspoon black pepper, and ½ teaspoon salt well. Cut the stems of peppers, and remove the cores and seeds.
2. Place the peppers in your bowl and toss them with oil. Wrap aluminum foil around the bowl securely.
3. Preheat the griddle to medium heat. Grease the griddle top with cooking spray.
4. Pour the egg mixture onto the hot griddle top Place the peppers on the hot griddle top and cook for 15 minutes.
5. Mix well the garlic, vinegar, and juices in a suitable dish.
6. Remove the peppers from your griddle and place them in a separate bowl, carefully covered with foil. Allow 5 minutes for the peppers to steam.
7. Scrape the charred skin off each pepper with a spoon. Quarter the peppers lengthwise and toss with the vinaigrette in a suitable mixing bowl.
8. Serve with a pinch of salt and black pepper to taste.

NUTRITION: Calories 170, Fat 13.1 g, Carbs 14.8 g, Protein 1.9g

183. Zucchini and Egg Plant Salad

Prep time: 15 minutes
Cooking time: 30 minutes
Servings: 4
Temperature: Medium-High

Ingredients:

- 3 tbsp. white wine vinegar
- 3 garlic cloves, minced
- 1½ tsp Dijon mustard
- Salt and pepper to taste
- 6 tbsp. olive oil
- 3 (8-ounce) zucchinis, halved lengthwise
- 1 red onion, sliced into ½-inch-thick rounds
- 1 red bell pepper, stemmed, seeded, & halved lengthwise
- 1 pound eggplant, sliced into ½-inch-thick rounds
- 3 tbsp. chopped fresh basil
- 1 tbsp. minced fresh parsley

Directions:

1. Whisk vinegar, garlic, mustard, ½-teaspoon salt, and ½ teaspoon pepper together in a large bowl. Slowly whisk in oil until thoroughly incorporated.

2. Measure out 2 tablespoons dressing and set aside. Add zucchini, onion, and bell pepper to the remaining dressing and turn to coat. Marinate vegetables for 15 minutes, tossing occasionally.

3. Preheat griddle to medium-high heat and brush with oil.

4. Place eggplant and marinated vegetables on the griddle, beginning with eggplant. Cook until charred and tender, 4 to 6 minutes per side, removing eggplant last.

5. Chop your vegetables into 1-inch pieces and toss with reserved dressing, basil, and parsley. Let cool for 10 minutes—season with salt and pepper to taste. Serve.

NUTRITION: Calories: 190, Carbs: 15g, Fat: 11g, Protein: 11g

184. Spicy Pineapple Slices

Prep time: 10 minutes
Cooking time: 15 minutes
Servings: 4
Temperature: Medium-High

Ingredients:

- ➢ 1 tbsp. butter, melted
- ➢ Salt to taste
- ➢ 4 pineapple slices
- ➢ 1/4 tsp chili powder

Directions:

1. Preheat your griddle at medium-high heat. Using butter, chili spice, and salt, brush pineapple slices.

2. Cook pineapple slices for around 5-6 minutes on each side on a hot griddle top. Enjoy.

NUTRITION: Calories 108, Fat 3g, Protein 2g, Carbs 21g

185.   Curried Cauliflower Skewers

Prep time: 15 minutes
Cooking time: 15 minutes
Servings: 4
Temperature: Medium

Ingredients:

- 1 cut into florets large cauliflower head
- 1 cut into wedges onion
- 1 cut into squares yellow bell pepper
- 1 fresh lemon juice
- 1/4 cup olive oil
- 1/2 tsp garlic powder
- 1/2 tsp ground ginger
- 3 tsp curry powder
- 1/2 tsp salt

Directions:

1. Whisk together oil, lemon juice, garlic, ginger, curry powder, and salt in your large mixing bowl. Add your cauliflower florets and toss until well coated.
2. Heat the griddle to medium heat. Thread cauliflower florets, onion, and bell pepper onto the skewers.
3. Place skewers onto the hot griddle and cook for 6-7 minutes on each side. Serve.

NUTRITION: Calories: 100 Fat: 8g Carbs: 6g Protein: 1g

186. Blue Cherry Brussels

Prep time: 15 minutes
Cooking time: 20 minutes
Servings: 4
Temperature: Medium

Ingredients:

- ➢ 1 (2 lb.) bag Brussel sprouts, shredded
- ➢ 8 slices bacon, thick-cut
- ➢ 4 garlic cloves, grated
- ➢ 1 tablespoon duck Fat
- ➢ 1 (5 oz.) bag dried cherry and walnuts for salad toppers
- ➢ 4 oz. blue cheese wedge
- ➢ Black pepper, to taste

Directions:

1. Grease the cooking surface of the griddle with cooking spray, and preheat to medium heat.
2. Place bacon on the griddle, and then let it cook until crispy. Combine the shredded Brussel sprouts, bacon, and bacon Fat in a mixing bowl.
3. Toss with a tablespoon of duck Fat or olive oil to coat.
4. Allow bacon to finish cooking and sprouts to become soft and slightly charred by tossing every couple of minutes. Add black pepper to taste.
5. Mix in dried cherries and walnuts, and cook within 1 minute. Top with crumbled blue cheese. Serve.

NUTRITION: Calories 318: Fat 15g: Carbs 14g: Protein 27g

187. Italian Zucchini Slices

Prep time: 15 minutes
Cooking time: 5 minutes
Servings: 4
Temperature: High

Ingredients:

- 2 zucchinis, cut into 1/2-inch-thick slices
- 1 tsp Italian seasoning
- 2 garlic cloves, minced
- 1/4 cup butter, melted
- 1 1/2 tbsp. fresh parsley, chopped
- 1 tbsp. fresh lemon juice
- Pepper, as needed
- Salt, as needed

Directions:

1. Mix melted butter, lemon juice, Italian seasoning, garlic, pepper, and salt in your small bowl—brush zucchini slices with melted butter mixture.
2. Preheat the griddle to high heat. Place zucchini slices on the griddle top and cook for 2minutes per side.
3. Transfer zucchini slices to the serving plate and garnish with parsley. Serve and enjoy.

NUTRITION: Calories: 125, Fat: 12 g, Carbs: 4.1 g, Protein: 1.5 g

188. Prosciutto-Wrapped Melon

Prep time: 10 minutes
Cooking time: 6 minutes
Servings: 4
Temperature: Medium-High

Ingredients:

- ➤ 1 ripe cantaloupe
- ➤ salt and pepper, as needed
- ➤ 8 thin slices prosciutto

Directions:

1. Cut the cantaloupe in half lengthwise and scoop out all the seeds. Cut each half into 4wedges, then cut away the rind from each wedge.

2. Sprinkle with salt and pepper, and wrap each wedge with a slice of prosciutto, covering as much of the cantaloupe as possible.

3. Bring the griddle grill to medium-high heat. Oil the griddle and allow it to heat until the oil is shimmering.

4. Put the wedges and cook until the prosciutto shrivels, browns, and crisps in places, 4 to 6minutes. Serve hot or at room temperature.

NUTRITION: Calories: 0, Carbs: 3g, Fat: 2g, Protein: 3g

189. Radish Bell Pepper with Black Beans

Prep time: 10 minutes
Cooking time: 13 minutes
Servings: 4
Temperature: Medium

Ingredients:

- 1 bunch of radishes, cleaned and grated
- ½ cup diced red bell pepper
- 2 cloves garlic, minced
- ½ cup cooked black beans, drained
- 1 tsp garlic powder
- 1 tsp onion powder
- Sour cream to serve
- Coconut oil or other cooking oil, as needed
- Salt and black pepper to taste

Directions:

1. Preheat the griddle to medium heat. Grease the griddle top with cooking oil.
2. Add the chopped red pepper and minced garlic to the hot griddle, then cook for 2 minutes. Transfer the mixture to a suitable bowl.
3. Stir in black beans, shredded radishes, garlic powder, onion powder, salt, and black pepper, and form a 12-inch-thick cake.
4. Cook the cakes on the griddle for 5 minutes per side. Top with a dollop of sour cream.

NUTRITION: Calories 116, Fat 2.3 g, Carbs 18.9g, Protein 6g

190. Lemon-Garlic Artichokes

Prep time: 10 minutes
Cooking time: 15 minutes
Servings: 4
Temperature: Medium-High

Ingredients:

- ➢ Juice of 1/2 lemon
- ➢ 1/2 cup canola oil
- ➢ 3 garlic cloves, chopped
- ➢ Sea salt, as needed
- ➢ Freshly ground black pepper, as needed
- ➢ 2 large artichokes, trimmed and halved

Directions:

1. Preheat the griddle to medium-high heat.
2. Combine the lemon juice, oil, and garlic in your medium bowl. Season with salt plus pepper, then brush the artichoke halves with the lemon-garlic mixture.
3. Place the artichokes on the grill, and cut side down. Gently press them down to maximize grill marks.
4. Grill for 8 to 10 minutes, occasionally basting generously with the lemon-garlic mixture throughout cooking, until blistered on all sides.

NUTRITION: Calories: 91: Fat: 28g: Carbs: 10g: Protein: 3g

191. Zucchini Spears with Sherry

Prep time: 5 minutes
Cooking time: 5 minutes
Servings: 4
Temperature: Medium-High

Ingredients:

> 4 midsized zucchinis, sliced into spears
> 2 springs thyme with the leaves pulled out
> 1 tbsp. sherry vinegar
> 2 tbsp. olive oil
> Salt and pepper, as needed

Directions:

1. Put all the fixings in a midsized zip lock bag, toss and mix it well until the zucchini are all coated.
2. Preheat your griddle to medium-high heat.
3. Remove the spears from the bag and place them directly on the grill grate. Make sure that the side faces downwards.
4. Cook for 3 to 4 minutes per side until you can see the grill starts popping up, and the zucchini become tender.
5. Remove from the grill and add more thyme leaves if needed. Serve and enjoy.

NUTRITION: Calories: 235, Carbs: 21 g, Fat: 16 g, Protein: 8 g

192. Sweet Potato Fries

Prep time: 10 minutes
Cooking time: 15 minutes
Servings: 4
Temperature: Medium-High

Ingredients:

➢ 2 tbsp. olive oil

➢ 2 lb. sweet potatoes, peeled & cut into ½-inch wedges

➢ Pepper & salt to taste

Directions:

1. Preheat your griddle at a medium-high and apply a thin layer of oil on top of the layer.

2. Toss sweet potatoes using oil, pepper, and salt in a large-sized mixing bowl—Cook sweet potato wedges for around 6 minutes on a heated griddle.

3. Cook within 6-8 minutes on the other side. Serve and enjoy.

NUTRITION: Calories 230, Fat 6g, Protein 4g, Carbs 40g

193. Griddle Spice Chickpeas

Prep time: 5 minutes
Cooking time: 30 minutes
Servings: 4
Temperature: Medium

Ingredients:

- 1 (16-ounce) can of chickpeas, drained
- ¼ cup olive oil
- 1 tbsp. ground cumin
- 1 tbsp. smoked paprika
- 1 tsp garlic powder
- 1 tsp onion powder
- 1 tsp kosher salt, + more to taste

Directions:

1. Combine all
2. Ingredients in a large bowl. Pour the mixture onto a cool griddle grill and bring the griddle to medium heat.
3. Allow the mixture to slowly come to temperature and continue to cook, frequently stirring, for up to 30 minutes or until crispy and crunchy. Finish with additional salt, if desired.

NUTRITION: Calories: 160, Carbs: 21g, Fat: 5g, Protein: 6g

194. Squash with Pesto

Prep time: 10 minutes
Cooking time: 10 minutes
Servings: 4
Temperature: High

Ingredients:

- ➢ 6 small summer squash, sliced
- ➢ Pepper & salt, as needed
- ➢ For the pesto:
- ➢ 1/4 cup pecorino Romano, grated
- ➢ 1 cup basil leaves
- ➢ 1 garlic clove
- ➢ 1/4 cup pistachios
- ➢ 1/4 cup olive oil
- ➢ 1/4 tsp chili flakes
- ➢ Pepper & salt, as needed

Directions:

1. Preheat the griddle to high heat.
2. Season summer squash with pepper and salt and place on a hot griddle top, and cook for 4-5minutes on each side.
3. Add all pesto
4. Ingredients into the blender and blend until smooth. Pour pesto over cooked summer squash and serve.

NUTRITION: Calories 116, Fat 10.3 g, Carbs 5.9 g, Protein 2.2 g

195. Portobello Caprese Stacks

Prep time: 10 minutes
Cooking time: 12 minutes
Servings: 4
Temperature: Medium-High

Ingredients:

- 4 Portobello mushrooms, stems removed & caps wiped clean
- 6 tbsp. olive oil
- salt and pepper, as needed
- 24 large fresh basil leaves
- 4 tomato slices (each about ¾ inch thick: 2 large tomatoes)
- 4 slices of fresh mozzarella cheese
- balsamic syrup for serving

Directions:

1. Brush the mushrooms with the oil, then sprinkle with salt and pepper on both sides.
2. Bring the griddle grill to medium-high heat. Oil the griddle and allow it to heat until the oil is shimmering.
3. Put the mushrooms and cook until well browned and tender, 6 to 8 minutes.
4. Transfer the mushrooms to a platter, gill side up. Cover the top with the basil: add the tomato slices, and finally, the mozzarella.
5. Return the stacks directly over the grill, close the lid, and cook until the cheese melts, 2 to 4 Minutes. Serve hot and drizzle the balsamic syrup.

NUTRITION: Calories: 195, Carbs: 22g, Fat: 8g, Protein: 12g

196. Maple-Cinnamon Carrots

Prep time: 10 minutes
Cooking time: 30 minutes
Servings: 4
Temperature: High

Ingredients:

- ½ cup maple syrup
- 1 tbsp. fresh ground cinnamon
- 2 lb. carrots (uniform in size, washed and peeled)
- 1 lb. thin-cut bacon
- pinch of salt
- 1 tbsp. finely chopped parsley, for garnish

Directions:

1. Whisk together the syrup and cinnamon in a bowl.
2. Lightly coat carrots with cinnamon-syrup mixture: a basting brush works well for this task.
3. Spiral wrap each carrot with one slice of bacon. Depending on the size of the carrot, two slices may be needed.
4. Apply another coat of the cinnamon syrup to the outside of the bacon and sprinkle with a pinch of salt.
5. Bring the griddle grill to high heat—Oil the griddle, and place the carrots. Ensure you lay the carrots with the tips of the bacon tucked under the carrots to prevent them from unraveling.
6. Reapply another coat of the cinnamon syrup, and cook additional 15 minutes or until bacon is crisp and carrots are firm but cooked.
7. Remove from grill, drizzle with any remaining cinnamon syrup, garnish with parsley, and serve.

NUTRITION: Calories: 70, Carbs: 9g, Fat: 3g, Protein: 3g

197. Bacon-Wrapped Zucchini Fritters

Prep time: 20 minutes
Cooking time: 15 minutes
Servings: 4
Temperature: Medium-Low

Ingredients:

- 2 cups zucchini, shredded
- 1/2 cup panko bread crumbs
- 1egg, beaten
- 1/2 tsp garlic, minced
- 1/4 tsp onion powder
- 1/2 tsp salt
- 1/8 tsp pepper
- Oil for frying

Directions:

1. Place the zucchini in a dry dishtowel and squeeze out as much liquid as possible.
2. Combine the panko, garlic, egg, onion powder, salt, and pepper in a mixing bowl. Combine the materials in a mixing bowl and roll them into golf-ball-sized balls.
3. Preheat the griddle to low or medium-low heat. Place some oil on the grill and then a ball of zucchini fritters.
4. Smash down a single sheet of parchment paper over the top of the ball with a spatula.
5. Allow the fritters to be brown on one side before flipping and browning on the other. Remove from the griddle and serve immediately with a ranch dressing.

NUTRITION: Calories 105.1, Fat: 2.8g, Carbs: 15.8g, Protein: 5.8g

198. Marinated Portabella Mushrooms

Prep time: 20 minutes
Cooking time: 15 minutes
Servings: 4
Temperature: Medium-High

Ingredients:

- ➤ 2 large Portobello mushrooms, stem removed & gills scraped
- ➤ 2 tbsp. olive oil
- ➤ 1 tbsp. red wine vinegar
- ➤ 1 tbsp. cherry blossom shoyu
- ➤ ¼ tsp salt
- ➤ ¼ tsp pepper
- ➤ 1 tbsp. butter

Directions:

1. Drizzle olive oil over the mushroom cap, then arrange top-down and season with pepper, salt, vinegar, and shoyu. Cover and marinate for 30 minutes in the fridge.
2. Carefully set the mushrooms on the preheated medium-high griddle, careful not to spill the marinade.
3. Place the butter in the middle of the caps and seal them. Allow for four minutes of cooking time. Remove the lid and continue to cook within a minute.
4. Using a knife or a bench scraper, slice the caps into pieces. The sauce will spill onto the griddle, making a massive sauce.
5. Cook for yet another minute, immediately remove from the griddle, and scrape up any remaining sauce if wanted.

NUTRITION: Calories 96, Fat: 10g, Carbs: 0.3g, Protein: 1g

200. Broccoli with Chili and Soy

Prep time: 15 minutes
Cooking time: 25 minutes
Servings: 4
Temperature: Medium-High

Ingredients:

- 6 oz. stem broccoli
- 2 tbsp. olive oil
- 2 tbsp. balsamic vinegar
- 4 tbsp. soy sauce
- 2 medium red chili, thinly sliced
- 6 tbsp. chervil., chopped
- 2 tbsp. sesame oil

Directions:

1. Set the griddle pan to medium-high heat. Brush the broccoli lightly with olive oil.
2. Cook the broccoli for 3 minutes on the griddle until golden brown, flipping occasionally.
3. While the broccoli is cooking, combine the remaining
4. Ingredients in a mixing bowl.
5. Drizzle the dressing over the broccoli and place it on a serving platter. Serve while the meal is still hot.

NUTRITION: Calories 294, Fat: 19.6g, Carbs: 27.3g, Protein: 8.9g

201. Griddled Asparagus with Zingy Lemon

Prep time: 10 minutes
Cooking time: 10 minutes
Servings: 4
Temperature: Medium

Ingredients:

- 2 cups asparagus spears
- 2 tsp olive oil
- 1 lemon, juiced
- sea salt, as needed

Directions:

1. Keep the woody tips of the asparagus spears for stock making. Lightly coat the spears with olive oil.
2. Place on a medium heat griddle for 2 - 3 minutes—Cook for the next 4 minutes after turning with tongs until lightly charred and soft.
3. Transfer to the serving plate, drizzle with lemon juice, and season with salt flakes if desired.

NUTRITION: Calories 38, Fat: 2.2g, Carbs: 4g, Protein: 2.2g

202. Cumin Chili Potato Wedges

Prep time: 10 minutes
Cooking time: 10 minutes
Servings: 4
Temperature: Medium-High

Ingredients:

- 1 tsp cumin
- 3 large russet potatoes, scrubbed & cut into 1-inch-thick wedges
- 1 tsp garlic powder
- 1/3 cup olive oil
- 1 tsp freshly ground black pepper
- 1 tsp chili powder
- 1 tsp kosher salt

Directions:

1. Set aside a small bowl containing the cumin, chili powder, salt, garlic powder, & pepper.
2. Preheat the griddle at medium-high on one side and medium on the other.
3. Brush the potatoes all over using olive oil & cook until brown & crisp on both sides, around 2 to 3 minutes per side, on the hot side of the griddle.
4. Transfer the potatoes to the cooler side of the grill, cover with foil, and cook for another 5to 10 minutes, or until cooked through.
5. Remove the potatoes out from the griddle and place them in a large-sized mixing dish. Toss the vegetables in the spice mixture to coat them.
6. Serve them warm and enjoy it.

NUTRITION: Calories 343, Fat 17g, Protein 5g, Carbs 42g

203. Zucchini with Parsley Mustard

Prep time: 10 minutes
Cooking time: 10 minutes
Servings: 4
Temperature: High

Ingredients:

- ➢ 1 tbsp. parsley leaves, chopped
- ➢ Salt and pepper to taste
- ➢ 2 lb. zucchinis, sliced into thin slices
- ➢ Olive oil to taste
- ➢ 1 tbsp. pink peppercorns
- ➢ 3 tbsp. mustard

Directions:

1. Preheat the griddle to high heat. Brush some oil on the griddle.
2. Season the zucchinis using salt and black pepper after brushing them with oil– Cook the zucchinis for 3 minutes on each side of the griddle.
3. Place the zucchinis on a serving dish after removing them from the griddle. Oil and season the zucchini is with pink peppercorns.
4. Place the mustard in a mixing bowl. Combine the parsley and mustard in a mixing dish and stir thoroughly. Serve the zucchinis with parsley mustard.

NUTRITION: Calories 90, Fat 2g, Protein 4g, Carbs 9g

Conclusion

By grilling food, you can enhance the flavor and nutritional value of your meal. Additionally, the higher heat levels used in grilling are more likely to result in a greater amount of vitamins and minerals evaporating into the food, enhancing its nutritional value and providing you with extra nutrients that are not available through other cooking methods like boiling or baking. In addition, you can enjoy delectable grilled meats without increasing your Calorie or fat intake because grilling does not require additional fat to cook the food.

Grilling may lower your risk for numerous chronic diseases, including heart disease, some malignancies, and type two diabetes. This is so that we can consume less Fat and Calories while still enjoying a filling supper thanks to grilling!

Nevertheless, grilling has more advantages. You are equipped to accomplish the task on your own, but you may use some help or direction from professionals. As a result, you should explore the dishes in this cookbook.

Copyrights Notice

Made in the USA
Las Vegas, NV
17 December 2023

82952432R20122